TWO
STRIKES
AND
OUT

TWO
STRIKES
AND
OUT

Edited by
WILLIAM E. McMAHON

COUNTRY LIFE PRESS CORPORATION
Garden City, New York

Editor's Note

THE EDITOR was a resident of Mexico from 1919 to 1938, serving first on the legal staff of Cia. Transcontinental de Petroleo, S.A., and then from 1932 until his retirement in 1938, serving as head of the legal department of Huasteca Petroleum Company. His work gave him direct and complete information concerning economic, social and political events as well as oil company-government relations.

This information, checked by a careful research and writing staff, is now published in an effort to present fairly and accurately the significant facts connected with the Mexican Government's program of confiscation of foreign-owned oil properties and to show the violation of the basic principles of international law dealing with property rights.

Because of their controversial nature especial care was exercised to present the most important phases of the social and economic problems of Mexico; the development and operation of the oil industry in that country and the labor controversy which served as Mexico's excuse for issuing the expropriation decree.

Woven into this record is the story of the operation of an American industry in a foreign country and its relationship to our domestic prosperity.

This book has been prepared for the purpose of helping create a clearer public understanding of the problems and threats which confront legitimate American business interests operating in foreign countries. The editor's hope is that this clearer public understanding yet will find a way to protect legitimate American property rights in foreign countries in order that American private capital will continue to flow into foreign investment channels.

The editor is convinced that there can be neither good neighbors nor domestic prosperity unless legitimate foreign trade and foreign investments are encouraged and protected.

William E. McMahon, *Editor*

Fort Worth, Texas
July 21, 1939.

CONTENTS

		PAGE
	EDITOR'S NOTE	iii
I	THE MEXICAN BACKGROUND	1
II	THE AMERICAN PIONEERS	24
III	LABOR MARRIES POLITICS	62
IV	THE SEIZURE OF THE OIL INDUSTRY . . .	89
V	"MEXICO KNOWS HOW TO HONOR HER OBLIGATIONS"	124

APPENDICES:

A.	MEXICAN RULERS SINCE PORFIRIO DIAZ	145
B.	INSURRECTIONS IN MEXICO SINCE 1910	147
C.	CHRONOLOGY OF THE CONTROVERSY OVER MEXICAN OIL	148

INDEX 155

TWO STRIKES AND OUT

CHAPTER I

The Mexican Background

IN THE SPRING of 1938, the government of Mexico seized arbitrarily the properties of foreign-owned petroleum companies operating within her boundaries, expelled the managements, proceeded to operate the wells with its own native personnel and to sell off the accumulated product. President Cardenas accompanied this act with a bland gesture toward payment. "We acknowledge the debt," he said in effect, "but we can't pay just now." Presumably, on some bright day, when Mexico was prosperous again, it would consider the troublesome matter of its debts. Meantime, Cardenas hoped that the men who managed these properties, and their governments, would possess themselves in patience. The outcome of earlier Mexican expropriations in lands and mines has proved how little a man or a company dispossessed on these terms can ever expect a cent in effective payment. Following these acts, the government sped up its policy of expropriating agricultural lands and began again to harass the important mining industry; the evident intention being to seize all profitable enterprises owned in whole or part by foreign capital and either to nationalize them or give them over to its allies, the militant labor unions, for operation on the co-operative plan.

Although the seizure of the oil properties involves the interests of other nations, conspicuously Great Britain and Holland, citizens of the United States are the chief victims, present and prospective, of the policies which Cardenas is following. Among all foreigners, Americans have always taken the greatest part in the development of Mexico and held the greatest stake. For another reason, the United States must sustain the main shock of the attack. The Monroe Doctrine binds her to protect all the Americas, including Mexico, from foreign aggression—a circumstance which President Cardenas doubtless took into account when he committed this act of aggression on his own part. Mexico is the northern outpost of Latin America, wherein American citizens have invested billions of dollars. Radical, nationalist and merely opportunist politicians from the Rio Grande to the Horn would like nothing better than an opportunity to stir up anti-Americanism. The United States has faced Mexican crises before. This is not only one of the most serious since 1866, when we joined with the republic to expel the Emperor Maximilian; it is also the most delicate. If the State Department lies down to Mexico we shall lose the respect of Latin American nations; if its policy be too brusque and belligerent, we shall lost their confidence.

For more than a century we Americans have maintained with Canada, our neighbor to the North, peaceful and even cordial relations; and mainly because Canada and the United States understand each other. Up to a near point, we have the same background of history. We speak the same language, play the same games, read the same books, appreciate the same jokes; our laws rest on the same basis and our governments have evolved from the same fundamental institutions. Most important of all, our national and individual psychologies are very similar.

We have had smaller luck with our Southern neighbor. There, the historic and racial backgrounds, the institutions, the very outlook on life, are as different as though Mexico, instead of bordering us on the Rio Grande, were cocked up on the edge of Tibet. They do not think on parallel lines with us, nor we with them. South of the border, incendiary politicians have used this difference of psychologies to create gross misconceptions of our intentions toward Latin America; and on our side, misunderstanding has caused many diplomatic blunders. Let us then, in preparation for dealing intelligently with a problem which may vex our foreign relations for many years, consider what Mexico is and what she is not.

Geography first: The country has about one-quarter of the area of the United States and supports about one-seventh of the population. Nature endowed it with an undue proportion of mountains. The great plateau of Mexico lies between two spurs of that lofty western cordillera which runs like a spinal column through the American hemisphere from Alaska to Cape Horn. These mountain ranges, plus a situation at the edge of the tropics, cause a great diversity of climate. As a native humorist once wrote of California, it never rains in Mexico and it always rains. In many of the plateau regions, as in that where the City of Mexico lies, the climate is Eden; in some of the coast districts, white men cannot live until they have cleared and sanitated tropical jungles. Some areas are capable of producing abundant and valuable crops just as they stand. Others with a fabulously rich soil can produce nothing until man brings in irrigation. In still others, peculiar conditions seem to defy nature; as Yucatan, which, having neither good soil nor moisture, found a generation ago that the fibre of a desert cactus could be twisted into the material for binding-twine and built up the profitable industry in sisal hemp.

Current literature on Mexico, and especially the variety emanating from the government, has described it as "the treasure house of the world" in mining resources. This is a poetic expression of a half-truth. Probably no mountains of the world ever held greater wealth of precious metals than those of Mexico in her primeval state. But long before the Spanish conquest the Indians had dipped into the richest and most easily recoverable deposits. After the Spaniards exhausted the accumulated treasure of the Aztecs, they began mining for themselves, employing methods but little advanced over those of their predecessors. Four hundred years of steady production have skimmed off most of the cream. There remain no "poor man's camps" where two miners with a winch, a bucket and a few tools can scoop out a small fortune in silver carbonates, or where sands sparkle with gold-dust and nuggets. Although Mexico still supplies the world with the greater part of its "new" silver and remains an important producer of gold, it is getting down to low-grade ores. Mining such deposits presumes large-scale operations, advanced skill in technicians and managers and heavy initial outlay of capital. As every mining engineer will tell you, it involves even more than that. Mining in remote regions usually resolves itself into a question of transportation. The ore may assay high; but building and maintaining roads, railroads, aerial trams, may eat up all of the profits. Even in our own Rockies, known deposits of high-grade ores lie undeveloped because of their inaccessible situation. And providing transportation, especially in a half-developed country like Mexico, requires much outlay of capital.

Another factor; probably large bodies of high-grade ores lie under Mexican soil, revealing their presence by no sign on the surface—almost all outcroppings have been followed up long ago. There, as in the United States, the era of the lone prospector with a pick and a burro has passed. Future exploration will involve much investment for speculative returns, combined with the very highest technical knowledge.

So long has the Mexican of the mountains delved in his native hills that the trade of mining runs in his blood. He has an instinct for uncovering the secrets of the earth. Mexican capital has not kept pace with him. It seems suspicious of investment in any form of heavy industry. When native capitalists do venture into mining, they tend to invest as individuals or families, not as stockholders. The extraction and treatment of low-grade ores and deep exploration call for large operations and large modern corporations. Also, while Mexico has many expert and efficient mining engineers, she has not enough. The American firms involved in the present crisis deal mainly with this kind of mining and are at present almost indispensable to the full prosperity of the industry.

The base metals, such as lead, copper and zinc, occur in the Mexican formations largely in combination with silver. When the chief value of a vein lies in base metals, it is never a poor man's proposition; its exploration and exploitation require large investment. In these metals, also, Mexico is still exceptionally rich. But in this instance, even more than in that of the precious metals, valuable deposits lie in regions at present too inaccessible for profitable mining. The same rule holds for iron and coal, the foundations of a modern industrial state. All tourists have heard of the mountain of iron at Durango; but for the most part this resource lies untapped. There are large deposits of low-grade coal and a certain, quantity of anthracite. This possibility of natural wealth has never been fully explored. Mexico has made only languid efforts to wed coal and iron and give birth to steel. The net result is three or four modest mills, the largest at Monterrey. Mercury and antimony have been returning profit to the mines for centuries and the deposits are by no means exhausted. In addition, there may be great possibilities in some of the rarer metals such as tin, tungsten, manganese and arsenic.

The last mineral resource to reach development, and the most important in this era, is petroleum. Mexican petroleum, like that of Texas, is "heavy oil." When first discovered, back in the last century, it had only limited value. Then came the use of crude petroleum for fuel purposes, the discovery of methods for extracting kerosene and gasoline from material of this type, and the world-wide demand created by the automobile and the airplane. When the industry began, Mexico had neither enough loose and courageous capital to exploit its deposits nor any oil-technicians whatever. The government and the laws of the time encouraged foreign enterprise, capital and experts. Dutch, British and especially American companies found the great fields of the eastern coast, drilled the wells, made the tropical jungle in which they lay habitable for man, built pipe lines to the ports, set up refineries for Mexico's domestic use, and developed an industry which became eventually the backbone of Mexico's export trade. In the course of time and compliant with new laws, most of the companies reorganized as Mexican corporations.

The greater part of Mexico's petroleum resources still lies undeveloped in the dark recesses of the primeval rocks. Two districts comprise all of the producing wells—that of the northeastern coast whose metropolis is Tampico, and that of the Isthmus of Tehuantepec. These, in the early 1920's, produced nearly a quarter of the world's supply. Bonanza discoveries since that time—notably in Texas, California, Oklahoma, Venezuela, Russia, Rumania and the Near East—have greatly increased the general output; and the harassing of capital by the government has reduced the Mexican. In 1937, Mexico produced little more than two per cent of the world supply. Spotted through the country from the Guatemalan border to the deserts of Lower California lie other areas where explorers have proved the possibility of deposits or where geologists have recognized the structures which usually contain petroleum. But several years ago new laws and ordinances so operated as to prevent exploitation of untapped deposits and to handcuff exploration. Even when, in the course of subsequent troubles, the Mexican government created its own agency, the enterprise interested itself not in development but solely in dipping into the deposits of the foreign companies by means of offsets. Since this account here is primarily concerned with the earlier development of Mexico, the government-created difficulties under which the oil companies operated will be treated in a succeeding chapter.

General Porfirio Diaz ended the decade of near-anarchy which followed Maximilian's downfall, and in 1876 became President destined to rule Mexico for a third of a

century. He took over a country where, owing to inept
government and constant revolution, most of the business
of life lingered in the conditions of the Seventeenth Century. It had primitive roads and virtually no railroads; it
farmed and ranched and manufactured by hand; its best
resources lay undeveloped. Diaz saw all this clearly, and
followed a vision of a modern state. He raised railroad
mileage from 500 miles to 15,000. The mines were still
worked with shovel and the winch; he introduced modern
equipment and methods. He built new factories and in-
stalled machinery in the old; he developed electric power.
At the end of his term Mexico produced most of the cotton
textiles which she consumed. All this required much
capital; and Mexico, like any other nation making the
transition into an industrial age, had neither excess and
liquid capital, the habit of investment nor, except in some
of the mines, technicians trained in modern methods.
Diaz followed the course necessary to a nation in such a
period of transition—he went abroad for his capital and
his technique, encouraging foreign companies, mostly
American, to explore and to invest. Americans and
Europeans constructed the dams which reclaimed arid
land by the hundreds of thousands of acres, developed
electric power, built the railroads and at first ran them,
gave manufacturing its start. More pertinently to the
present situation, during the latter years of this regime
American oil companies, at great immediate loss to themselves, made the explorations which revealed the rich
Tampico fields. When in 1910 Diaz, who had won his
power by revolution, fled the country before another
revolution, he had pulled Mexico across the threshold
of the modern era and seemed to have laid the basis for
a modern democracy.

And perhaps only seemed. "The strong man of Mexico," Diaz lived too near our own times for us to pass final judgment on his career. Toward the end of his rule, he professed that, dictator though he might be, he had been working toward a democratic republic, capable of self-government.

Diaz actually made little headway in establishing a democratic republic according to standards for such government which existed in the United States. However, his record should be judged, not in the light of our standards and our record, but in the light of standards and records existing in Mexico and the conditions he had to deal with. His task was an enormous one. One of his failures as judged from this late date was not to have provided education for the masses.

When Mexico broke away from Spain, literacy stood at one-half of one per cent. It increased, although slowly, during the first fifty years of independence. While there are no reliable statistics, at the beginning of the Diaz regime it had probably reached five to ten per cent. When Diaz departed, it had risen to fifteen or twenty per cent.

One thing above all others is necessary to a successful capitalistic democracy—a middle class. And the most stable element in any middle class is the independent farmer. Under Diaz Mexico attained a stability and order which she had not known since she won her independence. In these conditions, men here and there bought ranches or otherwise obtained a modest share of the public lands. Probably the proportion of land held in fee simple by dirt farmers who worked their own tracts was greater in his time than today.

Railroad construction and the growth of manufacture under Diaz's rule gave momentum to other social and eco-

nomic forces such as the development of oil fields by foreign companies, and large scale operations in the mines
had greatly increased the industrial element in the Capital
and in other large towns. During the period of ferment,
the workers began to form unions. Labor leaders and
radicals inspired the nascent labor movement in Mexico.
Generally, these drew their ideas and inspiration from
Europe, and especially from Spain.

The labor unionist of the European continent virtually
signs a manifesto of political faith when he receives his
card of membership. In Northern and Eastern Europe,
the unionists were at this period mostly Socialists who believed that the state should own the means of production,
while those of Spain were Syndicalists, holding to the
theory that companies of the workers should own and
operate their own industries. Syndicalism, carried to the
extreme, becomes anarchism; while socialism, when it
goes clear to the left, floats into communism. Yet to say
that all of the leaders who influenced Mexico in this period
were out-and-out Socialists or Syndicalists would be to
misrepresent the situation. Many of them followed a
vague native-American radicalism which had not yet
found its formulas or its full program. But they had all
borrowed from Europe the doctrine that labor unionism
must express itself in politics—mostly in revolutionary
politics. In Zapata's agrarian army of 1910–11, most
literate leaders carried in their kits a translation of
Henry George's *Progress and Poverty*. By 1915, Mexican intellectuals of the towns were reading Karl Marx
or Kropotkin. Born in a revolution, the Mexican labor
movement embraced revolutionary social doctrines in its
infancy.

The imported politicians, the labor leaders and certain ambitious agitators all intensified another disturbing tendency in the Mexican soul. Time out of mind, the demagogues of Latin America have used the United States as a punching bag. That catch-phrase, "The Colossus of the North," serves to remind audiences of our strength and richness and to raise up both national jealousy and vague fear; it is always sure of a hand. The Monroe Doctrine, which has prevented the Latin American countries from becoming a web of European colonies, becomes in the mouths of this gentry a denial of sovereignty and an intolerable affront to national pride. "Financial imperialism" is a phrase invented to describe the process by which certain European nations in their days of colonial expansion used investments, loans and development work as a screen for seizure of territory. By applying the term to the United States, the radical orator of the Southern hemisphere implies the policy. Even in the Argentine, where British investments outnumber all others from foreign sources, the soap-box speaker knows that he gets his best effect by attacking the "imperialism" of the United States.

Imported capital is a prime necessity for a pioneer nation breaking ground; on that point, Diaz thought soundly. While we of the United States were developing the West, we stood heavily in debt to European investors, especially the British. And elderly Americans remember the time when "the grip of England on our throats" was stock in trade with Populist orators. But with the borrowed money which built our railroads and developed our mines we accumulated domestic wealth. Eventually, the domestic capital supplanted the imported—as it always tends to do in the long run—and we passed from a debtor nation to a creditor. Exactly the same thing would have happened to Mexico under stable conditions and good management. Mexico had neither, and such stock phrases as "Colossus of the North" or "financial imperialism" were matches to light fires of resentment in a people just beginning its political thinking and lacking as yet any sense of discrimination between sound argument and sheer buncombe.

These changes in the social and economic life of Mexico soon created new political and governmental problems which in time fostered the creation of a revolutionary party. One of the leaders of revolt, Francisco I. Madero, presented the Plan of San Luis Potosi, which, for example, declared void the June 1910 election at which Diaz had been re-elected. Madero's Plan, which refused to recognize the Diaz government, so helped to crystallize sentiment against the aged ruler that the Diaz government was overthrown in May 1911. In November 1911, Madero became Provisional President of Mexico only to be assassinated sixteen months later. He was followed in office in swift succession by Lascurain, de la Huerta, Carbajal, Carranza, Gutierrez, Gonzalez, Chazzarro and Carranza again in March 1917.

In 1915, General Venustiano Carranza, who had for a year or so been boss of Mexico, openly assumed the Presidency and made it a virtual dictatorship. By now, politics had evolved to such a point that the ruler must keep his ear to the ground. No longer need the President conciliate merely the rival politicians with armed and pliant gangs at their backs; he must consider public opinion. But the threat from outraged public opinion did not consist, as in stable republics, in fear of defeat at the polls, because defeat at the polls too frequently served to create plausible grievances which raised the fighting instinct of the followers of the defeated candidate.

General Carranza, however, was in complete control of the situation and in 1917, a convention under his direction drew up a new Constitution for Mexico.

Although now amended in spots, this remains the fundamental law of the land. Later, we will consider the important and rather curious document in more detail. The articles most pertinent to this story dealt with subsoil resources. As regards all treasure lying under the surface of the earth—minerals and petroleum—it went back to the policy of the Spanish Kings. These henceforth belonged inalienably to the nation, no matter who owned the surface. The same principle applied to interterritorial waters, together with their banks. However, all surface and subsurface rights acquired before the adoption of the Constitution of 1917 were to remain private property, protected by law as such, and not to be confiscated or expropriated without just payment at the time of seizure. Any foreigner who acquired ownership in lands or waters or mineral deposits was to be considered a "Mexican citizen as regards such ownership" and, in case of controversy with the government, might not appeal to his own government for protection. This principle, known as the "Calvo Doctrine," began to assume special importance following the adoption of the 1917 Constitution.

All was set for confiscation; indeed, confiscation was already afoot. Zapata and other radical leaders had during the period of chaos seized large estates, driven out the *hacendados,* divided the tracts into small holdings among their followers. These were accomplished facts; and Roque Gonzalez, one of the ghost-presidents who ruled just before Carranza, had confirmed by decree the new ownership—at the moment he could not safely avoid this course. Carranza, when he came to power, went on with the process, although desultorily.

He had another prop for a shaky throne—anti-Americanism. In the European war he, the professed radical, took sides with reactionary Germany. Everyone knows of the German intrigues in Mexico which were the occasion, though not the cause, of our entering the World War and of our long watch on the Mexican border. Then, in 1920, came another of those Mexican revolutions, as suddenly hot and as suddenly burned out as a fire in a pile of loose papers; a bullet solved the Carranza problem. The "Sonora machine" succeeded—first Adolfo de la Huerta as Provisional President, then Alvaro Obregón with the strong Plutarco Calles sitting in his Cabinet as virtual boss, then Calles himself.

The movement toward distribution of the land proceeded jerkily, to an outsider somewhat insanely, and with almost total lack of economic foresight until Obregón came into power. The French encountered this problem after the Revolution. Napoleon Bonaparte solved it with his law of inheritance. No Frenchman might bequeath landed property according to his own whims and wishes; he must divide it among his natural heirs. In two generations, the French peasants boasted that every man who worked the land owned, or expected to inherit, a piece of it. When, in the years preceding the World War, the Liberal government of England decided to adopt the same policy, it accomplished its purpose by imposing heavy death-duties. But these were people with long political and social experience, working in periods of internal stability. The Mexicans, populace and politicians alike, were new to liberty. Also, they were living in a revolution, and all revolutions are in a hurry, and being in a hurry the Mexicans sought action rather than considera- tion of sound procedures. To an outsider, it would seem that they might have set aside a part of the huge public domain, cleared these lands for cultivation and then offered them at low prices to the landless while at the same time taking the long course with regard to the de- veloped estates. Obregón, like most Mexican rulers an opportunist, tended to strike instead at estates already in a high state of cultivation. Further, virtual blackmail by state governors or irresponsible political leaders vastly complicated the situation.

"Soak the foreigners" is a popular political policy in countries far more developed than Mexico. Obregón and his successors paid special attention to foreign holdings. Eventually, American citizens found themselves stripped of lands whose value mounted into the millions. The State Department protested, of course, and laid down the policy which it still professes to follow—"no expropri- ation without prompt and effectual payment." Mexico and the United States swung into a squabble over this wide difference of opinion; for a long period, we had no diplo- matic relations with Obregón. When representatives of the two nations finally sat down to talk business, Mexico set the precedent of pleading poverty. The American claim- ants, in common with the Mexican creditors, accepted at last a settlement which, with a solvent nation, would have been satisfactory. Mexico paid by handing to the claimants a special issue of bonds. Already even first-class Mexican government bonds, quoted on the New York Stock Ex- change at par of one hundred when Diaz departed, were falling toward their present level of one to one and one- half. Presently, these subsidiary issues became mere wallpaper. With a condescending flourish, the government finally made one apparent concession to holders of these bonds. The coupons would be recognized at face value in payment of taxes—which benefited only the few bondholders who had any Mexican property left. Also, a long process of squeezing foreign capital out of the railroads was already afoot. That is a complex story, the upshot being that foreign investors lost their stakes almost as completely as the land holders.

Obregón finished his term, and Calles openly took over a power which he had held half-secretly for some years. The strongest man who has held power in Mexico since Diaz fell, he was to use his strength ruthlessly in putting down an incipient revolution. Yet he had a sense of the possible, lacking in the other generals who dabbled with politics. And in his term another fire, lit long before under American citizens and long smouldering, burst into a blaze.

The Americans who first discovered the oil deposits of northeastern Mexico acquired their lands honestly and with fair title, according to the current laws of the land. So also did the British and the Dutch who followed them into the "Golden Lane." Even in the disturbed state of the country during the decade of constant revolution, between 1910 and 1920, they went ahead with exploration and development. By 1921, Mexico stood next to the United States in total volume of production. All Mexican administrations since the revolution of 1910–11 have tended to impose on this industry taxes as high as the traffic will bear; and during the years of chaos generals who were half-politicians and half-bandits held them up for special tribute. But when Mexico emerged into relative order, petroleum stood second only to mining as a source of direct taxes and furnished the principal item in Mexican export trade. Labor in the oil fields was growing expert; but native technicians or executives were lacking. Not even the ruthless Carranza dared confiscate an industry so valuable to the national economy and turn it over to the uncertainties of native exploitation. However, after the Constitution of 1917 decreed the nationalization of subsoil wealth, the companies had to put themselves on a different basis. To tell in full detail the troubles of the next few years would be wearisome, and at that the tale would be in spots incomprehensible to a reader who does not understand the Mexican laws, so different from our own. It is enough to say that through complex negotiations the foreigners, because of the firm stand taken by the American State Department, preserved their rights under international law.

Obregón, when he came in with a platform more radical than that of Carranza, began to make new passes at the foreign petroleum companies. Notably, he reorganized the government departments having jurisdiction over oil and set up a government-owned company which worked hand in glove with the government. Threats of seizure brought the "Bucareli Conference" whereat Mexico pledged the United States that it would pay in full and in cash for all expropriated property "prior to or at the time of taking." This stopped for the time being all proceedings leading toward confiscation. But exploration and development languished. Even the government-sponsored company showed no disposition to open new fields. Instead, taking advantage of the riparian rights granted to the state by the Constitution, it found ways and means to drill offset wells adjacent to the foreign holdings and to drain away their deposits—as though when you were drinking your lemonade through a straw another man dipped into your glass with his own straw. The foreign companies began to divert their capital to exploration in Venezuela and Colombia. From that time forth, Mexican oil production ran an intermittently downward course.

In the Calles administration the government threatened confiscation again. Relations between the United States and Mexico grew so frigid that another break seemed imminent. Then Secretary of State Kellogg sent Dwight Morrow to Mexico. The Mexican government was slow to recede from its untenable position. But when he finished, he had persuaded Calles to agree that the subsoil regulations should not be applied in a retroactive sense and had made arrangements by which the companies might continue to operate their wells, pipe lines and refineries in comparative security. More than that, perhaps, he inaugurated an era of good feeling between the United States and Mexico.

The honeymoon was brief. All this time, new influences were driving Mexican public opinion further toward the left. The Russion Revolution and the establishment of the Soviet Republic had given extreme radicals all over the world a focus, a program and a seasoned doctrine. Communists filtered into Mexico—some of them freelances, some of them, doubtless, Russian agents. Nothing in the modern world is more obscure than the actions of this gentry; and our generation will never know their exact methods in Mexico or the extent of their operations. We know only that they were following the traditional Communist policy of infiltration and of tearing down democracy, including the capitalistic system essential to it. We have a revealing glimpse now and then—as when an American mining engineer, inspecting a railroad car which his own train had wrecked, found it loaded with Communist pamphlets.

Presently, a regularly organized Communist party appeared. Leon Trotsky, the man without a country, appealed for asylum in Mexico. It did not matter that he was the arch-heretic of that Soviet Russia which so many Mexicans were beginning to admire. He was an extreme social revolutionist—that was enough. The labor unions were growing powerful and cohesive; and, of course, the Communists paid them special attention. It became noticeable that they usually put their emphasis not on higher wages but on irritating and sometimes impossible demands in regard to working conditions. Except among peoples with long political experience, revolutions never stop with their original objectives. The Mexican revolution was following this rule. There were counter-currents too. The Fascist nations and other foreign elements were at work here and there, as secretly as the Communists, raising eventually the dim possibility that Mexico might become another Spain.

Calles ended his term in 1928, as provided by the Constitution, but he picked his successors by hand and sat on the lid in the background. When Lazaro Cardenas took over in 1934, Mexico was enjoying a boom in business; but decades of loose political and financial management had undermined the foundations. Already, the defaulted interest on nearly a billion pesos of government bonds had mounted to a point where it almost equalled the principal at par. The government could not borrow money abroad and could borrow at home only by force. Fear of confiscation and of interference from the government hung over all Mexican capitalists. Never much inclined to put their surplus money into anything so intangible as stocks and bonds, they grew more hesitant than ever. The decline in oil production, wholly due to governmental policy, was whittling away a rich source of public revenue. The methods used to distribute the land had produced one unexpected result. Indian corn is the wheat of Mexico—the staff of life. Ex-peons, handed a slice of the large estates, tended to lie down on the job. On part of their lands, they raised enough corn and beans to feed their families, their chickens, and perhaps a cow or a pig; and then let the rest lie fallow. A country with large areas of fertile and undeveloped land was beginning to import Indian corn in order to feed its people.

Just before he left the Presidency, Calles announced a Six-Year Plan of internal improvement and social reform and had the Constitution amended to give the President a six-year term. The wording is significant; Mexicans had heard of the Russian Five-Year Plan and using Soviet phraseology had become good politics. The country was swinging to the left and Cardenas swung with it. Presently, Calles seemed to be trying to put the brakes on his protégé's over-hasty reforms. Therefore, Cardenas arrested his old leader and exiled him. Busily he began building dams, improving roads, running power lines. Still more busily he expropriated and nationalized private property. Before long, he felt the pressing need for money. At about that time, Vicente Lombardo Toledano, hitherto merely a professor, a very radical intellectual and an incendiary orator, became the man of the hour in Mexican labor and the unions moved toward the left. Here was a situation of which an opportunist might take advantage— on the one hand a new, ready-made machine to stiffen his following and back him up in any drastic measure, on the other the possibility of seizing the rich oil properties of the eastern coast and selling both their accumulated supply and their current production. That might tide his government over the crisis. This may have the appearance of reading the dictator's mind, but his actions prove that he must have thought in some such terms.

The rest is not background but current history. The first stage was a strike in the oil fields, for higher wages— the petroleum companies were already paying by far the highest wages in Mexico—and, perhaps more important, for other concessions so absurd that they seem to be borrowed from a fantastic comedy. The company which met them would not only have forfeited its profits but probably have ceased altogether to produce oil. A series of legal actions brought the question of justice in these demands before that Mexican bureau which corresponds to our Labor Relations Board. It decided brusquely and arbitrarily in favor of the strikers. The companies appealed to the Supreme Court. The Court, by now a convention of yes-men for the President, decided exactly as expected. The companies announced that they could not produce oil on those terms. Whereupon, Cardenas put into effect a decree of expropriation, the law which authorized it had been passed two years before by way of holding a club over the foreign companies, and seized the properties. This, according to Toledano, was his intention from the first. This act, like most of the others which led up to it, was patently illegal. Every sound lawyer in Mexico knew that. The British and Dutch governments protested indignantly. Ignoring the Dutch, Cardenas answered the British by breaking off diplomatic relations. This dumped the situation into the lap of Uncle Sam. Taking advantage of the fact that the official correspondence was not made public, the Mexican government spread the report that the United States government did not object to the confiscation.

Finding the process easy, Cardenas moved on to expropriate still more agricultural lands owned by Americans and to make hostile gestures toward the mines. The American notes grew stiffer. The replies from Cardenas became defiant, even sneering. Before that disturbed summer of 1938 ended, he was saying in public speeches that any man who started a business in a foreign country must take orders or get out, leaving his property behind; and as regarded the oil properties he had ceased to mention payment in any practical form even in a remote and hazy future.

Meantime, the reckless course he was steering had brought him among dangerous shoals. As witness an episode which, although it reached some of the American newspapers, attracted little attention. In the summer of 1938, a period when the gold and silver reserve behind Mexican currency was strained almost to the breaking point, a consignment of newly printed government notes arrived at Mexico City from New York. They looked like the regular and familiar paper money. They had been in circulation for several days before anyone but the bankers noticed that, by a little overlay on the plates, the engravers had eliminated the promise to redeem in cash. The sale of "forfeited" oil had not been enough. Mexico had started down the long, dark trail of inflation.

*　　*　　*

These last paragraphs are merely a brief summary of an adventure in public chicanery which involved a dozen major legal processes, varying from subtle to insolent in their defiance of the written law and the moral law, as well as a score of slippery political intrigues. Before we tell that story in detail it seems necessary for the sake of clarity to go back and deal more fully with the background of the two chief protagonists—the foreign petroleum companies and the Mexican labor unions.

CHAPTER II

The American Pioneers

THE STORY of Mexican oil is in its earlier passages only a chapter in that absorbing romance, the development of oil in our own West. Even when Mexico remained a personal possession of the Spanish Emperor, travelers and geographers recorded ponds and pools of that mysterious, rather forbidding substance, bitumen—later and more popularly called asphalt. This, we know now, is only petroleum, thickened or hardened by contact with air; and these pools are usually the outcroppings of a large subsurface deposit. But from the time of Marco Polo, who first reported lakes of pitch in Asia, until the middle of the Nineteenth Century, petroleum lay in the ground almost useless to man. A Scottish engineer found in the 1850's that he could distil from oil shale—rock impregnated with petroleum—the inflammable liquid called at first "coal oil" and then "kerosene." A German invented a lamp to burn it for domestic uses. Then Colonel E. L. Drake, an American, discovered that a sluggish, inflammable, ill-smelling liquid oozed from certain hills in Pennsylvania. The Indians and afterward the whites had used it as a liniment for rheumatism, and quack doctors were bottling this "Seneca oil" as a cureall. He identified it as the inflammable component of rock shale and reasoned that the seepage indicated a large deposit in the

24

earth below. So he rigged a crude drilling apparatus and in 1859, struck oil at a depth of sixty-nine feet. By benevolent accident, those Pennsylvania fields yielded very high-grade petroleum with a paraffin base. Distilled—as yet crudely—into kerosene, it drove out whale oil and candles as domestic illuminants. In Pennsylvania, oil men learned their trade so thoroughly that for more than half a century discoverers of new fields in any part of the world sent for American experts.

Gradually the chemists of the distilleries began to discover the by-products of petroleum so important to modern industry—lubricating oils for example, and paraffin wax. One of these was for a long time only a bother and embarrassment. The first process of distillation yielded a light, volatile liquid which emitted highly inflammable fumes. These became explosive when mixed with air. We termed it "gasoline;" the British, "petrol." Distillers could sell a little of it as "naphtha," an effective but dangerous cleansing compound. The rest they threw away. Then someone invented a gasoline stove. Although giving a hot, instant flame, it was not fool-proof. It did, however, put this curious substance on the commercial map.

Then, during the last decade of the century, Europeans worked out the gasoline engine, which capitalized the explosive quality in the fumes of that liquid. In 1895, Rudolph Diesel built an internal-combustion engine of the type named after him. Other inventors harnessed the gasoline engine to a carriage and turned out the first expensive, unreliable automobiles. At about the same period, power-engineers began to realize that crude oil was in many circumstances superior to coal as a generator of steam.

That was the situation in 1900, when the history of the American oil business in Mexico really begins. At the moment, the world supply of petroleum probably ran near to current demand. The automobile remained a rich man's toy and an unsatisfactory one at that. There were less than five thousand in the United States. Industry was showing itself most reluctant to install fuel oil in place of coal. The man who at that time sank his capital in developing new oil fields had to be an optimist—he must believe that the gasoline engine would eventually supplant the horse in land transportation and that crude petroleum, not coal, would furnish the power both for sea transportation and for many steam-engines. The oil prospectors at the turn of the century all held to that fantastic illusion. So did a bicycle repairman of Detroit, named Henry Ford.

In 1893, a period when our rich mid-continental fields of the United States still lay undiscovered, California struck oil in the Coalinga fields. C. A. Canfield, a veteran and expert oil prospector, had staked his small fortune in this bonanza and won—as had E. L. Doheny, a young oil man from Wisconsin. Both belonged to that old type of Western mining man who thinks of a big strike only as a stake for new strikes. President Diaz of Mexico was moving energetically to develop the resources of his country. Mexico was short on experts; he was importing both from outside of the country. He had begun with railroads, and A. A. Robinson, American, had taken charge of the Mexican Central. The government had compelled or persuaded him to run a spur line eastward from San Luis Potosi across the Eastern cordillera of Mexico and down through a jungle-country to the coast at Tampico. This was the best harbor in northeastern

Mexico; about it sprawled a small and poverty-stricken city tributary to a few unimproved wooden wharves. The country which the line traversed was only lightly productive—a little mining in the mountains, a little cattle-raising in the foothills, a few tropical products in the clearings of the jungle. Robinson realized that this road would never pay until someone developed the region. He began to study its natural resources. Presently he heard from ranchers and peons of bitumen pools, of hills that oozed liquid pitch.

He had lived long enough in Mexico to know that it was being prospected, though on a small and hesitant scale, for petroleum. As far back as 1876, a Yankee sea captain, finding a surface pool of bitumen near Tuxpan, had raised some capital in Boston, drilled a well and got a very modest flow of petroleum which he refined on the spot into kerosene and sold in the surrounding towns. This company failed. So did a few others which got only a trickling, unsatisfactory flow or no results whatever.

In the 1890's, London was the world center for mining of all kinds and British capital especially venturesome. A company which included Cecil Rhodes and Lord Cowdray among its backers had dropped nearly a million dollars in exploration with little luck. Its prospectors were working south of the Tuxpan River on the eastern coast—as we know now, just at the southern edge of the great northeastern deposits. Experts looked over the British operations and reported to London that the formations were shallow and unpromising for large operations; whereupon the British pulled up stakes and began to explore the Isthmus of Tehuantepec where, a few years later, they made great discoveries. And that, except a little blind, venturesome, and unsuccessful wildcatting, tells the story of Mexican petroleum up to the Twentieth Century.

Robinson believed that a real discovery in the territory about Tampico would solve his problem. With Indian guides cutting a way, he did a little exploring and found that some at least of the stories about pools of pitch were true. Then one of those little episodes with great results clinched the matter in his mind. When he built the railroad, the government had given him a detailed map whereon were lettered the local place-names not only of hamlets, rivers and mountains but of hills and gulches. And he noted how often these names—such as "El Chapopote," "El Chapopotal," "Chapopotilla," "Oja de Breo," "Cerro de la Pez," and the like—were synonyms for tar or pitch. This trifle decided him. He had heard of Canfield and Doheny as first-class oil prospectors who now had money and were willing to take a chance. With an invitation to visit Mexico as his guests, he sent his own inexpert report on the prospects of oil about Tampico. He was making a stronger appeal than he knew. From pools of oil and bitumen like these, the pioneers of Coalinga had traced the course of the great Californian deposits. The California oil men accepted his invitation.

A member of this party has recorded their despair as their train crossed the cordillera and dipped into the hot, swampy, rainy jungles of the coastal strip. Looking at it with the practical eyes of the pioneer, they remarked to each other that a man would scarcely try to mine gold in a country like that—let alone oil. Making an oil field pay would involve settling an industrial population, laying pipe lines, creating shipping facilities and finding markets. They were in this discouraged mood a week later when, with Indian guides showing and cutting

the way, they rode thirty-five miles west of Tampico to
Cerro de la Pez ("Pitch Hill"). And there, they forgot
everything except the glow of the prospector who has
made a strike. This was not a mere pool; it was a great
spring, bubbling forth sluggish streams of petroleum.
That same day, they identified a second exude. Joining the
exploring party, engineers and geologists traced these
spots of bitumen through a hundred miles of jungle, and
gained a rough idea of the formations. It was, they reported, a "big proposition." It had to be, in order to
return profit from a country so remote and so difficult.

This pioneer Mexican Petroleum Company bought
or leased its lands outright as did the companies that
followed it. Constantly, critics of the American oil
companies in Mexico have asserted that they obtained
their landholdings through "concessions" from President Diaz. Both in spirit and in letter, this statement is
untrue. In order to encourage the oil companies to take
the risks of exploration and development Diaz did,
indeed, exempt the early companies from taxation until
such time as they reached commercial production. A
thousand American cities, trying to attract new industries,
have followed the same policy; and we call it enlightened
municipal practice. The British companies received a few
concessions in the following circumstances: When finally
they got headway, they found some promising deposits on
terrenos baldios or public lands, owned by the government. Here, they proceeded to do business on the plan
which many American oil companies follow when they
discover oil on privately-owned land in the United States.
They agreed to give the government, as owner, a "roy-
alty"—a fixed percentage of the gross product or its
equivalent in money. They paid high in the end for these

concessions. Diaz insisted that, as a pledge of good faith, they invest part of their capital in Mexican federal bonds. And those bonds, bought at about par of a hundred dollars, in 1938 rated on the stock exchange at about one dollar.

But the Americans made no discoveries on public lands. When the nascent Mexican Petroleum Company found that spring at the base of Cerro de la Pez, the managers hunted up the owner and bought his ranch outright. They could not conceal their motive, and they did not try. The seller quite understood that these Americans wanted it for the oil rights and, having no faith whatever in petroleum as a business, was glad to sell for what he considered a fancy price. And here, it is necessary to expand a paragraph in the preceding chapter.

Civilized nations follow—speaking generally—two variant theories concerning subsoil rights to land. The United States, most colonies of the British Empire and several other nations, hold that the owner of the surface has the right to everything below the surface down to the very center of the earth. With us, and in general with the other countries which follow this theory, he who finds paying ore under unclaimed public lands may, upon proving his sincere intention to work his claim, receive title to a limited area on the surface and to all that underlies it. Mining is the most speculative form of business. The man who pioneers in it must expend much time or money or effort—or all three—on a prospect which may end with a mere hole in the ground. This policy of the English-speaking nations has encouraged the legitimately adventurous spirit and is the main reason why the Americans and British lead the world in mining.

The other and opposite theory covering ownership of subsoil rights, which is a relic of absolute monarchy, is usually compromised in practice partly because it will not work and partly because of varying interpretations and misconceptions concerning its definitions and limitations.

This latter reason, the misconception concerning its definitions and limitations, is the basic cause of most of the problems which arose to plague the foreign-owned oil companies in Mexico. This ghost of unreality took official form in the attempts of Mexican officials to make retro-active the provisions of Article 27 of the 1917 Constitution. This article directly declared that all subsoil rights of hydrocarbonates belonged to the nation.

The official as well as the popular Mexican justification for investing Article 27 of the 1917 Constitution with retroactive qualities is the direct descendant of the old Spanish "Law of Reversion" and that Mexican law, rest-ing on the Spanish law, therefore holds and has held, since independence was gained from Spain in 1814, title to sub-soil rights.

In the first place this is not true because the Kings of Spain never owned the subsoil rights on lands privately held; in the second place, the sovereignty of the Spanish King ceased when Mexico gained her independence, there-fore under the rules of international law the King's politi-cal rights and prerogatives also became extinct.

It is possible that the general misconception concerning the Spanish law on surface and subsoil rights arose during the Spanish regime in the Americas and that it came from the confusion which resulted from technical and other irregularities of authorities in Latin America when they issued land grants. As a result of these errors or irregularities many persons occupied lands in excess of the area granted to them. In an effort to clear up this situation, the Spanish King issued his decree of October 17, 1754, the terms of which directed that his representatives in America require all occupying lands to come forward and produce their titles so that they might be confirmed. He ordered further that those who occupied land in excess of what their grants called for would have to pay for the excess and thereby obtain confirmatory title for it. The King's order to the authorities in the Americas read as follows:

> They [the authorities] shall issue in my royal name the confirmation of their titles by which the *possession and dominion* of said lands, waters or Valdios [sic] shall be legalized, so that at no time whatsoever shall the owners or their successors, universal or particular, be disturbed therein.

The term "dominion" referred to in the royal order of 1754, in connection with the titles to be confirmed thereunder, meant full, absolute ownership in the land in the same sense as Americans understand the term "fee simple title."

Thus royal pronouncement illuminates the controversy regarding Mexico's justification for attempting to give retroactive properties to Article 27 of the 1917 Constitution and it shows clearly that her claims rest upon thin air. The only rule of property which Mexico could have inherited from the Kings of Spain definitely and completely invested subsoil rights in the surface owners.

On December 4, 1786, the King of Spain promulgated his celebrated *Ordenanza de Intendentes* for New Spain, by which name Mexico was then called. By virtue of Article 81 of that ordinance, *intendentes* and other authorities were directed to proceed with the sales of land, and the confirmation of titles, and in doing so they were to be guided by the royal order of October 15, 1754, above mentioned.

The clarifying action which completely disposes of the Mexican contention that subsoil rights had belonged to Spanish Kings was defined by royal order of King Charles III of Spain on November 28, 1789, in which he proclaimed definitely and finally that subsoil rights are invested in the owner of the land.

The occasion for this royal order was created when Gaspar Melchoir Jovellanos took the position in a controversy with the Director of Mines of Spain that coal underlying privately owned property belonged to the landowner thereof and not to the King. In his arguments supporting this contention Señor Jovellanos said that:

> Under the fundamental, primitive common law [*ley comun*] of Castile, mines do not belong to the royal patrimony but are the property of the King's vassals, free, allodial and perfect, and that they embrace the subsoil as well as the surface of the lands, and that all rights appertaining to the dominion belong exclusively to the landowner *without any reservation in the King;* and that the incorporation by the King into his patrimony of mines in private property is not based on any *reserved right in the King* but upon that supreme authority which is proper to and inseparable from sovereignty to provide and order what is necessary for the preservation of the state, and to which all persons, all properties, and all private rights are subject.

King Charles III was not departing from established legal procedure when he issued the royal order concerning the Jovellanos contention because under the celebrated code of laws, the *Siete Partidas,* which was applicable to all of lands under Spanish rule, private property could only be taken for the King's use or for public purposes, and when it was taken for such purposes just compensation had to be made for it.

Since, under the rules of international law, the sovereignty of the Spanish King ceased when Mexico gained her independence, so also under the rules of international law, did the King's political rights and prerogatives become extinct. Thus there was no carry-over of old royal rights in the new republic. Therefore, even assuming the Spanish King might have had any unusual property rights or prerogatives there could have been created no method by which such illusory rights could be passed on to Mexico with the change in sovereignty. Mexico could hold its territory only subject to its own Constitution and laws and under that legislation land tenures have been individualistic and protected by constitutional guarantees. Careful search and comparison of the five Constitutions under which Mexico operated between her first one in 1814 and the adoption of the 1917 Constitution will reveal that Mexican law, as did the Spanish law, made subsoil rights the property of the surface owner.

A distinguished Mexican jurist, Licenciado M. G. Villers, in his treatise on Article 27 of the Mexican Constitution of 1917 stated that "From the moment in which the nation was constituted and declared its independence, it announced by implication that all of its rights as a nation and as a sovereign and independent state came into being with its own existence, and were not derived from any other state, nor by any act of donation or alienation which other peoples and authorities, equally sovereign, may have made to it."

The Mexican people adopted their Constitution on October 22, 1814, during their war for independence. This was followed by the Constitutions of October 4, 1824; of 1836;

of June 13, 1843; and of 1857. Each of these Constitutions contained safeguards to private property. Each expressly declared that private property could be taken only for a public use and upon just compensation. There is extant no authoritative ruling of a Mexican court, made while those Constitutions were in force, which failed to render due respect and observance to the constitutional mandate for the protection of private property rights.

The oil companies did not begin to meet with serious difficulties in occupying and operating the land they had bought or rented until after the adoption of the 1917 Constitution whose Article 27 read:

> The ownership in the lands and waters comprised within the limits of the national territory belong in their origin [*originariamente*] to the nation, which has had and has the right to transmit the dominion in them to private persons, thus constituting private property.
>
> Expropriation can only be made for causes of public utility and by means of indemnification.

The language of this seemed clear. The dynamite in it became evident when the government attempted to make this provision retroactive as to subsoil rights and thereby make it apply to all property which had been acquired prior to the adoption of the 1917 Constitution. From that date forward foreign oil companies operating in Mexico have been beset with difficulties.

The managements of the foreign-owned oil companies in Mexico were beset with other difficulties some of which arose from certain peculiarities of Mexican law which made the purchase of land a less simple process than in the United States. Most important, the law provided that all the owner's heirs must approve the transaction. Occasionally, the owner had concealed the existence of a left-wing heir or two; more often, when a piece of otherwise valueless land spouted suddenly a million barrels of oil, some faker would arise to claim kinship with the original owner. Further, in this remote, difficult region careless or corrupt authorities had often ignored the niceties of the law in giving title. Claims arising from these sources brought much blackmail and troublesome lawsuits; and from them sprang a persistent report that American titles were faulty. Most transfers of Mexican land incurred in those days the same risk; but American titles to oil lands were as good as any. By chance, most of the land in that northeastern coastal district was held in tracts comparatively small for Mexico—*ranchos,* not *haciendas.*

As happens after any strike, the news ran like wildfire through the oil business. Other Americans, some wildcatters and some with the backing of established companies, began exploring that region between the Tuxpan and Panuco Rivers and throwing out feelers into the country north of the Panuco. The British began opening up their district on the Isthmus of Tehuantepec; the Dutch followed in. Within the next fifteen years, scarcely a major oil company in the world omitted to take a shot at those formidable jungles where gangs of laborers must clear the way with machetes ahead of geologists.

Oil prospecting, if not actually in its infancy, had not yet grown up. The outcroppings of bitumen gave the one sure sign; but science still understood so imperfectly the geology of petroleum-bearing formations that experts could not with any certainty follow such a pool to its source. The best prospectors, like Canfield, seemed to work by a sixth sense—"a nose for oil." The very apparatus they used was primitive from the standpoint of 1938;

the deep-drilling methods which have opened up the rich fields of western Oklahoma and Texas were still many years away. In these circumstances, individuals and companies sank money by the hundreds of thousands of dollars in dry holes or, having at equal expense discovered oil in promising quantities, discovered also that they could never command the capital to get their product profitably to market, and quit. Only three or four of the pioneering American companies ever came through to stable profits. They did it not because they had much initial capital but because their directors and promoters had skill in raising still more money. And, above all, had old-fashioned American nerve.

The story of the early oil business in Mexico is not only a romance but a string of romances. There was exploration in the coastal jungle with "its hot, humid climate, its apparently incessant rains, those pests the *pinolillas* and *garrapatas* (wood ticks), its dense forest which seemed to grow up as soon as cut down, its great distance from any center that we could call civilization, and still greater distance from any source of oil-well materials." So, later, wrote a pioneer in a mood of pessimistic reminiscence. The men who succeeded with Mexican oil were the ones who faced these conditions and went ahead nevertheless. It must be, they realized, a large-scale job. First, they had to make this jungle habitable for white men and for native Indian labor. For it harbored a pest more dangerous than wood ticks—malaria. Had the discovery occurred ten years before, this enemy alone would have driven out the pioneers. But by now science knew that the anopheles mosquito is the carrier of the disease; and the American Army, cleaning yellow fever out of Havana, had taught us how to deal with mosquitoes. After the first discovery, transportation is the key problem in mining, whether for metal or petroleum. The single-track railroad would be both expensive and inadequate to deal with production on the scale which they envisaged. But there lay Tampico, a good harbor, though unimproved. It was a natural outlet to the best markets—the Atlantic coast of the United States and Europe. Very well—improve it with wharves and warehouses! That outlet would make necessary regular lines of ships. All right—get them! Some of the best prospects lay a hundred and fifty miles from Tampico. This meant sinking a fortune in pipe lines. The steady demand for kerosene and fuel oil in Mexico, the small but growing demand for gasoline, would furnish a market whenever their chemists found satisfactory methods for "cracking" this heavy Mexican oil—a problem not solved for years. So they must eventually build refineries at Tampico. They lacked a sure foreign market. Very well; educate engineers, railroad men and manufacturers along the rich Atlantic coast of the United States to the advantages of fuel oil over coal. Final task and perhaps most important to the story of oil in Mexico: All this time they would be moving a new industrial population into this sparsely settled district. Therefore, they must provide civilized housing.

It did not all happen at once. In fact, this fundamental work went on for years before successful oil companies even began to approach the black side of the ledger. To take one example, the first well drilled almost experimentally at Cerro de la Pez proved a "gusher." Further exploration established the probability that the drillers would encounter mostly wells of this type. Before opening them up, it was necessary to build either tanks,

reservoirs or pipe lines to accommodate their sudden
flow. In spite of Doheny's persistent propaganda on
behalf of fuel oil, the market developed very slowly.
Until 1906, indeed, it scarcely grew at all. The old Standard Oil Company probably saved the pioneer Mexican
Petroleum Company when it laid an order for two million
barrels a year for five years. Experiment and calculation
showed that the current method of shipping oil in barrels
was expensive, wasteful of space, cumbersome. So these
Mexican operators became largely responsible for the
oil tanker, now such a familiar character of sea lanes and
ports all over the world. That involved a problem in
designing so as to eliminate the danger of a "shifting
cargo." It was solved.

Financing the enterprises, however, constituted the
chief problem. Very soon, all the successful companies
had exhausted their funds and were appealing to the
investing public or to the bankers. The failure of some
early companies, the operations of blue-sky promoters,
had made judicious investors cautious regarding Mexican oil stocks. When it came to loans, the chief security
being supplies of oil still lying underground, the American banks were at first no more enthusiastic. The pessimists had plenty of arguments on their side. When the
first of the successful companies entered Mexico, they
established contact with the geologists of the Diaz government. These men had looked over the region; and all
but one, Professor Ezequiel Ordoñez, had reported
unfavorably. In the subsequent controversy, Ordoñez
resigned his position in the government and took service
with an American oil company. American engineers, sent
by the bankers to survey the region, returned more
optimistic reports. But when asked to state in dollar

values the quantity of oil certainly in sight, they made such cautious estimates that the banks would not lend enough money to finance operations so gigantic. Finally, bankers came down to see for themselves and to consult the company geologists. New and promising deposits had been located in the meantime. The bankers went away ready to underwrite bonds.

The Americans brought in their first producing well in May, 1901. Not until ten years later did the surviving companies feel confident of success. At that, production had risen only from 10,000 barrels in 1901, to the comparatively modest figure of 12,000,000 in 1911. But they were ready to go. And by 1921 the yearly output had risen to 193,000,000 barrels*—that was the banner year.

And gradually they worked transformation on the northeastern coast of Mexico. Settlements with modern conveniences surrounded the greater wells. Wide ribbons of cleared land, bordering the pipe lines, ran over mesa and jungle. Tugs, towing barges, navigated streams where in 1900 the only craft were dugouts and canoes. Settlements had grown into prosperous towns. The metropolis of Tampico showed the greatest change of all. In 1900, it was a remote, sleepy little port which existed to ship the scanty production of the back country—such staples as hides, woods and sassafras. Surrounded by swamps and lagoons, it was prey to epidemics. Housing was primitive; sanitation did not exist. A decade later, it had sewer systems, electric lights, a water-filtration plant and modern housing. American experts had seen to the drainage and oiling of the swamps in order to destroy

---

*This is the most conservative estimate—the one followed by the Encyclopaedia Britannica. Other authorities set the figure at 202,000,000 barrels.

dangerous mosquitoes. Streets of substantial business blocks ran along the water front. A sand-bar had made passage into the harbor impossible for deep-draught vessels; so American engineers dredged a channel. For all that, Tampico and especially the tributary region, had in those days the atmosphere of an old-time mining camp. As in early-day San Francisco, Deadwood, or Virginia City, the bands, dancehalls and cafés blared all night, money flowed like water, the air seemed to quiver with optimism, men venturing into the back country wore the law in leather on their hips, and here and there conflict blazed into "rough stuff." In time, fictionists discovered this fertile ground for romance, and the kind of American who gets his culture from the magazines, if asked in an association test to name three Mexican cities, would begin "City of Mexico—Tampico."

Most important of all, however, was the rise in the standard of human life. Up to the border of the oil district ran at first the peonage system for labor. Inside of that border labor worked under free conditions. From the beginning, the companies paid wages "as good as the best in Mexico." After they went over the top, they paid by far the highest wages—a fact which even the most ardent Mexican exponent of confiscation has never denied. A job in the oil fields became the chief ambition of the native laborer. It being necessary to house an industrial population, the companies did the work thoroughly. The workmen who flocked to the region of Tampico came usually from mud huts thatched with grasses— somewhat like the hogans of our Navajo Indians. They found themselves eventually living rent-free in comfortable brick or wooden houses, usually with pure running water, often with electric lights.

Going further, the companies established free medical service for all employees and their families, and later built hospitals on the same terms. Less than ten per cent of the children in Mexican rural districts had ever seen the inside of a schoolhouse. Wherever these Americans built a settlement to house their employees, they built also a school large enough to accommodate every child belonging to their workers. Usually, too, they paid for its maintenance; and year in and year out, these were far superior to the government schools in abutting regions—when such existed. No son or daughter of an oil worker in the eastern Mexican fields longed in vain for an education. Some of these benefits were only a response to new social laws. But in most cases, the companies had either anticipated the law or, when it was passed, gone beyond its provisions. In most cases, native Mexican manufacturers employing large labor forces ignored government regulations in this respect. The foreign oil companies not only obeyed but went the lawmakers one better. The same motives impelled the companies to install libraries, halls and fields for recreation in every town or center where any considerable number of their employees lived. The enlightened marvelled especially at the efficiency and success of these Americans and Britishers in preserving public health. Through them, indeed, the idea of modern sanitation first entered Mexico.

By 1910, there was no longer any need to worry much over markets. The idea of fuel oil was taking root. Manufacturers were adapting their plants, shipping firms their engines. When four years later Europe went to war, the coal-burning warship was becoming as obsolete as the trireme. Refiners had solved the problem of extracting gasoline from heavy oil. Henry Ford had perfected his "poor man's car" and was turning it out as fast as he could build factories. Passenger cars had begun to crowd the streets; the motor-driven commercial truck had appeared and was driving out the draft horse.

But just at the moment when the dreams of the pioneers seemed to be coming true, the storm broke over Mexico. There followed five or six years of virtual anarchy with Presidents, Provisional Presidents and dictators chasing each other through the Presidential palace. All were generals. Most of them won their way to power by the sword; many of them perished by the sword. Armies ranged Mexico, some the ordered legions of revolutionary politicians, some the followers of generals who were revolutionists for banditry only. Here and there, bands of peons invaded the great *haciendas,* drove out the owners, looted the mansion-houses and divided the lands among themselves. Some of the revolutionary generals, and especially those of the bandit type like Pancho Villa, not only shot all prisoners but all political opponents whom they could catch. President de la Huerta courted trouble in another dimension when he provoked the United States to such a point that our Navy occupied Vera Cruz. When, on top of that, Villa began raiding across our border, a foreign war seemed almost inevitable.

In this chaos, the busy, prosperous region about Tampico stood an island of comparative order and stability. The oil companies, having opened up their discovery at long last, were cashing in on a decade of unprofitable work; and month by month the exports of Mexican petroleum shot upward. To this period belongs the episode of "Cerro Azul No. 4," still a wonder-tale of the oil business. A stretch of high grazing land, varied with spots of jungle, lay about eighty miles southwest of Tampico. When the prospectors looked it over, they found that black pools, their edges striped with the white bones of cattle which had mired themselves in bitumen, sprinkled the whole area. No Indian of the region went willingly near the Cerro Azul (Blue Hill). It passed as dangerous and of bad omen.

Such signs, and the geology of the region, indicated to the company owning this land that it held a major deposit, and before drilling "for business" it spent years in preparations. Also, just in case of unexpected emergency, the engineers threw up tanks and created a temporary reservoir by running dirt walls across an arroyo.

The emergency came. On the night of February 9, 1916, the drillers struck gas. When two days later they resumed drilling, they touched off a rush of oil that had almost the force and fury of an explosion in a munitions dump. At Juan Casiano, sixteen miles away, people mistook the noise for a clap of thunder. Tools and fragments of the derrick were blown so high that when they landed, one of them embedded itself sixteen feet deep in the earth. Not only the derrick went, but the heavy machinery already set in place to cap and control the flow. Within a day the column of black oil rose to a height of 600 feet; within a week the tanks and emergency reservoir held 260,000 barrels of oil. It was nine days before, by an operation whose daring ingenuity is a tradition even to this day, the American engineers and their Mexican mechanics succeeded in putting a valve over the base of the column and making a connection with the pipe line. In less than six years, "Cerro Azul No. 4" produced 57,000,000 barrels.

This is still a world's record; but all over the fields of Tampico and Tehuantepec other wells with a less sensational flow were mounting up oil production for Mexico. Every year they multiplied and remultiplied the modest 12,000,000 barrels of 1911. The European war created a frantic demand for gasoline, fuel and lubricating oils. No need to worry over markets any longer. But some worry over getting enough shipping! That the companies accomplished all this in the midst not only of a world war but of an amorphic civil war, seems now something of a miracle. The answer, probably, lies in their enlightened labor policy. Their employees were not peons but free laborers working at wages and in conditions unknown elsewhere in Mexico. A thousand small establishments had sprung up to meet the needs of these flush workers in the oil fields. Mexican business, in that region, wanted no revolutions. And whatever President ruled in Mexico City, the government still showed an intelligent reluctance to kill the goose that was laying the golden eggs. For the period of exemption had passed; and oil production, now heavily taxed, was contributing vitally to the federal revenues.

That, however, was not the only revenue which the oil industry paid to Mexican politics. Now and then, a bandit-general would swoop down on to the district, take possession of a set of wells or a whole field and demand tribute under penalty of driving out the working force or destroying the plants. Both threats came to the same thing. An oil well may be as powerful as a cyclone, but it is also as delicate as a watch. Letting it run too fast or too slowly, or stopping operations altogether, may bring in that ruinous salt water which is the personal devil of the oil producer. The companies paid up, after a little bargaining, just as the sensible citizen forks over when a highwayman pokes a gun into his face.

The most serious episode of this kind happened, however, in 1923, after Mexico had emerged from chaos to a state of comparative order. A general descended upon the "Golden Lane" with forces large enough to occupy the whole district. He asked for a large ransom on the same old terms and under the same old penalties. This time the situation presented special difficulties. He was an enemy of the established government. To pay up might be considered an unfriendly act. On the other hand, if the government sent down forces to squelch him, he could before his defeat or retirement damage American and British property to the tune of tens of millions of dollars. The American companies consulted the State Department in Washington. It advised them to pay. But first, in order to keep the transaction open and aboveboard, they put the case to the Mexican government. Somewhat to their surprise, it gave advice which, freely translated, ran: "You're held up and the cheapest way out is to get the best terms you can from him. We won't hold it against you." This episode lay forgotten for more than a decade. Then, when the Mexican government of 1937 began to rationalize the seizure of the Tampico oil fields, it bobbed up in a new dress of airy invention. The "American oil magnates," it appeared, had used their money to finance a revolution! Holding on in those days required personal courage. For one long period, the United States and Mexico had no diplomatic relations, and our State Department was advising all our citizens to leave the country. The American oil men sent their families home and grimly carried on.

But 1917, which brought a brief period of relative calm to Mexico, brought also the beginning of more serious trouble. Carranza had blasted his way to the Presidency. An astute opportunist politician, he played the old, sure-fire tune of "foreign domination." Touching on the oil companies he added an accusation of "swollen profits." Denouncing foreign corporations, especially those of the United States, had, he found, popular appeal. He and his followers harped this tune until they nearly wore out the strings. That slogan is still ringing through the soft airs of Mexico; and this, perhaps, is the place to discuss what values the oil business, in the hands of American, Dutch and British companies, has taken away from the country and what it has given.

"People have put more money into the ground than they've ever taken out of it," runs an old saw of the mining game; and any candid mining engineer would probably tell you that it is true. Mining, whether for gold or base metals or oil, is a speculative business. The discoverers and promoters spend money and toil to develop a region in hopes of a bonanza. Some strike it rich; and we have in extreme cases such fairy-tale properties as Comstock Lode in silver, Homestake in gold, Anaconda in copper. The public hears of them but not of the enterprises which never returned a dollar in gross returns. Yet our Rockies and Sierras are filled with abandoned prospect holes, the hollow, sunken monuments to failures in mining. Change the terminology a little, and you have the story of oil in Mexico. In that early era of discovery and development, company after company failed to strike oil in paying quantities or could not raise enough capital for the expensive development work necessary in this difficult field, and folded up "leaving its money in the ground." The ones which staggered through the pioneer era produced enormous quantities during the booming period. But most of them entered this era with a large deficit; and the heavy revenues of a few good years left no great margin of profits. Veteran oil men who have followed these Mexican operations from the beginning are nearly unanimous on two points. First, only three or four companies have consistently made money. Second, take it all in all, the foreign investors in Mexican oil have in bulk just about broken even.

The books of these companies which quit and were dissolved have long ago gone to the junk man; and so no one can cite figures for the early years. But in 1937, when Mexican politicians were moving to appropriate the foreign-owned oil business, the companies submitted their accounts to an eminent, neutral and highly esteemed firm of auditors. These experts reported that the net profits of the whole foreign oil business in Mexico averaged, in the decade just past, four and one-quarter per cent per year. The calculation was based not on watered stock, but upon a capital structure amortized and adjusted to the terms of the depression years. Those are not "swollen profits."

Let us, however, take that rate of profit as a basis for determining what the foreign-owned oil companies have taken out of Mexico, and what they have left in the country. In the course of those years, labor-cost has been probably the biggest item of expenditure. This includes not only wages, the highest ever paid in Mexico, but the housing, educational services, medical care and recreational facilities already described. Almost every peso of that money remained in Mexico. Next in order of importance comes the necessary expense of machinery for the

wells and refineries and for kindred materials such as
pipe lines. Mexico has no facilities for making machinery.
If Mexicans had owned these enterprises, they also would
have been obliged to buy their machinery and heavy
materials outside of the country. The same applies to
sea transportation. Mexicans do not build ships; having
at present no steel industry of any consequence, they
cannot. As far as possible, the companies have bought
their small and current supplies in Mexico; Mexican oil
companies, as well as American, Dutch and British, would
have been obliged to buy the rest outside of the country.

Finally comes that large item, in some ways the most
important of all—taxes. From the moment when any of
the wells began to produce, both federal and local governments piled taxes on to the oil companies. Since the
late 1910's, taxes on petroleum have stood next to those
on metal mining as the chief source of federal revenue;
but for them, Mexico might have collapsed long ago.
Naturally, this money stayed at home. The new, hard-
finished main roads, which the American motor tourist so
much admires, were largely paid for from the taxes on
petroleum and loans from the oil companies. From the
same source, directly or indirectly, came the money for
many another permanent addition to the wealth and comfort of Mexico.

Then there is the minor item of executives and
experts. These men—well paid, of course—were in the
beginning Americans, Britons or Hollanders. Partly
through merit, partly on orders from the government,
many native Mexicans trained in schools of mining or in
the industry itself have come to occupy salaried positions.
But most of the men at the top were foreigners. These
usually worked under long-term contract and settled

down with their families. Therefore, they spent most of their pay in Mexico. A few Mexican investors held blocks of stock in the companies which fought their way to success in the creation of wealth, which since the earth's formation had lain unused and unusable. Through the combinations and recombinations which usually occur in a growing industry, these companies have generally become subsidiaries to larger concerns. The Mexican investors, as a rule, travelled along with the foreign stockholders and kept their stake in the oil business. And they, of course, shared in the dividends.

Because President Diaz was a realist first and foremost, he wasted no time or effort in trying to develop his country's oil resources either with government funds or with companies owned exclusively by Mexicans. The government did not have adequate funds. His government, or the private corporations under his wing, would have found it necessary to issue bonds and to sell them abroad. For Mexico had very little liquid capital and had not yet developed the habit of corporate investment. He could scarcely have borrowed at a more favorable interest-rate than four and one-quarter per cent, which, as has already been shown, was the average yearly profit of foreign companies between 1927 and 1937. And his own people would not take the risk. Neither his people nor the Mexican officials knew anything about the oil business.

In choosing the other course Diaz and José Limantour, his financial genius, played a long and prudent game. To develop the oil resources of Mexico on the domestic plan, they would have found it necessary to import foreign experts capable of taking charge of the undertaking because few, if any, Mexicans of that period had had any experience in large corporation management or in the highly specialized business of finding and producing oil. Also, it was a gamble; let foreigners take the risk! After a third of a century, the fact remains that the development of the oil business in foreign hands has taken no more money out of Mexico than domestic exploitation would have done. The oil companies have lived up to all of their obligations. And they left fully ninety per cent of all gross receipts in Mexico in the form of wages, freight costs, royalties, taxes, extensive improvements, such as refineries, pipe lines, equipment, housing, etc. So much for the "bleeding of Mexico" by alien oil corporations.

This story has run ahead of its chronology. Back, now, to 1915–17, when General Carranza, as "first chief," was coming into power, pledged to fight the foreign corporations and to redistribute the land. Such policies were not readily adaptable to the old Constitution ratified in 1857 and amended under Diaz. For this reason—and also by way of emphasizing his break with the past—he set lawyers to drawing up a new one. Radicals, including a few foreigners, helped out with advice. Passed by Congress and ratified by the states with the speed which a virtual dictator can command, it went into operation on May 1, 1917. We have already described those articles affecting the oil business—the return to the royal Spanish principle of dividing surface and subsoil rights and the virtual nationalization of claimed mineral resources. They even nationalized the beds of dry streams and legalized the act by the claim that water flowed in them during the rainy season and thereby made them a part of the nation's inland waterway system. The foreign oil men felt the ground slipping out from under their feet and black uncertainty began to settle like a spray of new oil over the

Mexican fields. The cantankerous Carranza was applying his anti-American policy by giving aid and comfort to German plots and plotters as the United States was now at war with Germany. It was possible that Mexico might come in against us. The new Constitution, with its radical revision of all laws of property, might prove a formidable weapon in his hands. True, it ordained categorically that the property laws should not be applied in a retroactive sense, and that titles to mining lands so acquired before 1917 were good for all time. But this Constitution could easily be amended; and Carranza had already hinted that his eventual aim was the nationalization of all production.

On the verge of their producing fields, the companies owned other areas as yet undeveloped. Geological understanding of petroleum-bearing formations had advanced mightily since 1901. The explorer locating oil had no longer to depend on surface-seepage such as pools of bitumen. The operators knew for a practical certainty that these lands overlay rich deposits. Since an oil well, once drained, does not renew itself, the continued prosperity of an established company depends upon opening up new supplies. This, in the fields about Tampico, would involve spade-work of the same old kind—clearing jungles, building towns to house employees, running pipe lines, drilling exploratory wells at $75,000 to $250,000 apiece. No man of foresight was especially keen to take such a risk when his petroleum deposit might at any time be knocked out from under him.

Even in face of this, exploratory and development work did not stop at once. But it dwindled constantly—took a new drop with each of the crises which were to mark the coming years. In 1917, however, many areas already opened up were coming into full yield, and for four years the petroleum production of Mexico increased deceptively. In 1921, as said before, it reached the all-time peak of 193,398,000 barrels, and Mexico rated as the second oil-producing country of the world. Fluctuatingly, the output now decreased. In 1937, after an upward surge caused by some unexpected yields in the British-owned fields, the country produced 46,907,000 barrels, but it had fallen to seventh place. Yet more—very much more—recoverable petroleum still lies under the soil of Mexico than has ever been extracted. One cause alone accounts for this decline—a blight on exploration.

Mexican petroleum was at this period a matter of lively concern to the State Department of the United States. We were engaged in a world war which ran by fuel oil and gasoline. Also, we were entering a brief era when economists were growing increasingly anxious about the shrinkage of our own oil reserves. We could not then anticipate the discovery of new and even greater domestic fields; and the deep-drilling methods which have so multiplied production in recent years were not yet invented. We were a national market for Mexican oil exports. Anything that stopped or greatly diminished this supply might have serious effects on our national defense.

In spite of the straining relations with Mexico, our State Department asked Carranza's intentions. He referred us to the non-retroactive clause in the Constitution and assured us that the articles regarding subsoil ownership "would in no way prejudice present property rights." A breathing spell until the summer of 1918. Then Carranza issued his decrees laying down the conditions under which prospectors or companies might explore or produce in Mexico. They included a rule that a company must obtain a "drilling permit" before it could work old deposits or look for new ones. Not only did this limit prior rights, but experience led the oil men to expect that this was going to be a cumbersome process, marked by delays and red tape. Nor was experience disappointed. The chilling thing, however, was the manner in which it was done. Carranza's remarks at the time hinted that Mexico considered these persons as interlopers to be ejected when the country got round to it. This, of course, put a further crimp into exploration.

However, Carranza did not last much longer. He had promised to bring heaven all at once. He could not even start that general distribution of the land by the promise of which he had inspired his armies. Another of those hair-trigger revolutions broke out. Generals Obregón and Gonzalez, coming down from the North, drove him from the city. He took the route to Vera Cruz, traditional for Mexican political fugitives; but his enemies caught up with him, killed him. Mexican political chronology for the next fifteen years is a confusion of regular Presidents and Provisional Presidents. But the underlying situation is simple enough. The "Sonora Triumvirate" of Obregón, de la Huerta and Calles had formed a machine which held supreme and almost unchecked power.

As stated before, Obregón, who came to the Presidency in 1920 and served out his term, proceeded energetically but irregularly with the division of land. He seemed to have followed no consistent plan, except that of political expedience. Whenever the spokesmen for any sufficiently large and especially clamorous body of ex-peons demanded an estate, he yielded, expropriated the property, and either organized it as an *ejido* or divided it among them. Naturally, his followers paid special attention to foreigners. American after American whose glory was a ranch run on modern methods, and who considered himself a permanent resident of Mexico, lost his all. During part of this period the Harding administration did not recognize the Mexican government. There were unofficial exchanges of views, nevertheless, and then open negotiations. Finally, in spite of vacillating but often ruthless policy on the southern side of the Rio Grande and occasional inept or blind diplomacy on the northern, the parties to the dispute established certain principles and attitudes which have ever governed our controversies over property held by Americans in foreign lands. First, Mexico admitted that the articles of the Constitution regarding surface rights to land should not be interpreted as retroactive. In other words, titles acquired before 1917 still stood. Presidents, Ministers of Foreign Relations and the Supreme Court have since affirmed that principle again and again. Second, we admitted that any nation has the right to expropriate property, but only if it makes "prompt, assured and effectual payment." That principle is not an American creation. It is written into international law. On this basis the land claims were "settled." That is, Mexico pleaded poverty, as she was to do again in 1938. She paid the old bill with bonds which soon became dogs and cats. The principle, however, remained unchanged.

Also, the controversy over rights to oil lands reached a temporary settlement, although an unsatisfactory one. The Supreme Court of Mexico had in 1921 affirmed the principle that all land or land-rights legally acquired before May 1, 1917, were private property under the Constitution. The article of the Constitution nationalizing subsoil rights was, it declared flatly, not retroactive and does not affect pre-existing rights legally acquired.

It confirmed this by four more decisions to the same effect. As regarded oil claims, however, it added the condition that the owner, before that vital date, must have performed "positive acts" proving his sincere intention of producing oil by doing development or exploration work.

That phrase "positive acts" was hazy and susceptible to invidious interpretation. Indeed the Mexicans began at once to interpret it in that sense. Another diplomatic row ended with the Bucareli Conference of 1923 between representatives of Mexico and of the United States. Our stronghold was the fact that we were not recognizing the Obregón government, which Obregón himself much desired. We won there a seeming victory. The final agreement, as signed by both parties, provided that "positive acts" included not only drilling in the subsoil but entering into any contract regarding its uses and also the purchase or lease of lands for the evident purpose of producing oil.

Yet in the face of this, when Calles assumed the Presidency, the Mexican Congress proceeded to ordain that the oil companies must hold their lands not in fee simple, but under "confirmatory concessions." The companies objected. The order went, however. The government issued a certain number of these concessions, then seemed to lose interest. Holders of many producing areas never received them. They worked on nevertheless, still basing title on the plain language of the Constitution.

Already the government had begun to pile on more taxation by adding production and export taxes. This seemed admirably to serve its purpose of increasing revenues; but any export tax tends to blight the industry upon which it is imposed. Finally, about 1923, came well-authenticated reports that the government intended to set up or to back a government-owned or controlled petroleum company which, presumably, would have a monopoly on exploration and development of new fields. It was the last straw. After that, little new foreign capital ever came into the Mexican oil business. The whole world was swinging into the boom period of the 1920's and the demand for petroleum and its products was increasing even beyond imagination of the pioneers. Capital was in a mood to take chances. But not in Mexico. The new enterprises, the old concerns with world-wide interests, generally flocked to newly opened fields—in our hemisphere, mostly to Venezuela where the government was stable, the laws fair and liberal. Knowledge of oil geology had made great advances since 1901; and oil prospectors had established to the satisfaction of experts the existence of wholly untapped Mexican deposits in regions where no one had ever yet seen an oil derrick. But they remain undeveloped even to this day.

As prophesied, the government-sponsored company was organized with a flourish. It was more than a corporation; it worked hand in hand with the National Administration of Petroleum Control, which is as though our Anaconda Copper Company also amounted in practice to the Bureau of Mines, Interior Department. In any controversy with a rival, it could always count on a favorable decision. Financially, this company never amounted to a great deal. It intended to raise capital in Mexico. But Mexican investors were just as suspicious as foreign bankers of petroleum operations with the hand of the government upon them. Government finances were in a bad tangle. It could therefore expect little backing from the Treasury. Exploring and preparing to produce in a

Mexican field is, as shown before, a long, hugely expensive process. The various government organizations therefore began dipping into the subterranean deposits already acquired, explored and developed by foreigners.

By way of explanation it may be stated that here and there nature has trapped pools of petroleum at varying depths below the earth's surface. The oil rests there in sands or other porous rock formations. Outcroppings of rock or other surface structural indications serve as guides in helping geologists find likely locations on which to drill wells. The usual custom of oil companies is to purchase or lease the oil rights of the land adjacent to the location for the well. Otherwise others, without sharing in the heavy exploration costs, can sink wells in the proven area and extract as much oil as the original discoverer. Further, salt water at the bottom of the formation is the ticklish factor in the extraction of petroleum. Inexpert work at any point may cause a churning which mixes water and oil in a valueless emulsion or makes the petroleum deposit unrecoverable; and the most sensitive point of all is the edge of the layer of petroleum, where it lies thinly above the water.

But the Constitution of 1917 gave the government, either federal or state or both, absolute, inalienable right not only to the country's waterways, inland seas and lakes but also to their beds and banks. No one has ever believed that the Constitutional Assembly introduced this article as a joker, but in the hands of the government company it became such. These eastern rivers are spotted with lagoons, lakes and brooks. The rest was easy. Drillers for the Mexican company took possession of banks or dry beds, sunk wells, and proceeded to extract oil by millions of barrels. Under the laws of Mexico, at the time when the companies purchased the land, they had the absolute right to the petroleum in these deposits. Further, the millions of dollars spent in exploring them and getting ready for production gave a moral right. But when they protested to the proper and competent authorities, almost invariably they met a prompt and final refusal to intervene.

Finally: Although by now the country had developed many experts in the various branches of oil production, the government-sponsored company suffered from that chief limitation of a commercial venture under the thumb of politicians—the preference for executives with political influence over those of proved technical achievement. So again and again the management ordered wells drilled on that delicate edge of the petroleum layer, and with disastrous results to both their company and to its competitors.

It is not possible to calculate the millions of barrels of oil virtually stolen by this process and added to the taxes which the Mexican government was exacting from the foreign oil producers. One can only guess at the value of oil, still lying in underground deposits, which these blunderers ruined. But this is certain—these companies, founded to develop the oil resources of Mexico and so add to the national wealth, merely whittled away the resources and decreased the wealth. And at that, the venture ended in bankruptcy!

But the foreign companies staggered on somehow. The Calles group held power for more than a decade of comparative peace, broken now and then by the necessity for putting down a brief rebellion; and Plutarco Calles was probably too much of a realist to believe that public operation of all the oil fields would yield more revenue than the heavy taxes on the foreign producer. The Mexican Treasury was going constantly further and further behind the game; and he could not prudently do any juggling with one of its main assets. But Mexican public opinion, much influenced by the social experiment in Russia, was drifting steadily to the left; and he seemed forced now and then to make toward the oil companies a gesture amounting to a slap in the face. Ambassador Dwight Morrow, as already related, achieved in 1927 a live-and-let-live compromise involving not only the petroleum problem but other commercial questions which had been causing friction between the two republics. Again, Mexico —this time through President Calles himself—affirmed the principle that all titles to oil lands good before 1917 were good for all time. He had the petroleum law amended to this effect. Further, Congress confirmed the definition of "positive acts" contained in the Bucareli Agreement.

Now, with harmony restored, North American tourists began to "discover" that next-door neighbor about whom, before that period, the average American knew and cared less than about Egypt or Iceland. And notably, at about this period the oil question seemed to disappear from our newspapers. It was a deceptive truce. The trade knew that the exactions were growing, and that new and disturbing factors had appeared. Chief among these was a set of labor unions whose leaders seemed less concerned with getting better hours, wages and conditions for their followers than with ultra-radical politics. This movement merely crept until the end of 1934, when Lazaro Cardenas succeeded to the Presidency. Then it went with a rush. Cardenas proceeded to repudiate and exile Calles, his political teacher and master; to bring radicalism behind him by a platform which hinted constantly at collective ownership of the means of production on the Marxian plan; and to make new and extensive appropriations of private property in lands, factories, and utilities. Not until 1936 did he get around to that large and difficult proposition, oil; and even then he opened with an indirect fire from these political labor unions which were becoming his strongest allies.

Which introduces the detailed story of labor unionism in Mexico, insofar as it relates to the confiscation of oil properties.

CHAPTER III

Labor Marries Politics

T HE UNITED STATES, Great Britain and most of the
European nations entered the industrial era early in
the Nineteenth Century; in Mexico, the transformation did not even begin until the 1880's, when Diaz solidi-
fied his rule and found himself able to go ahead with his
plan of a modern, scientific and self-contained national
economy. Mexico made the same initial mistakes as the
other nations and with the same long and disturbing consequences.

At length, in the days when power had begun to slip
from the hands of the aging Diaz, a small group of intellectuals with Socialist or Syndicalist opinions began underground organization of the workers.

The Flores-Magnon brothers were the most able leaders in this element. Sometimes from hide-outs in Mexico
itself, sometimes from the United States, whither in 1906
they had fled in fear of their lives, they managed to start
a strike in the Cananea mines. It was a violent affair—at
least twenty men killed, buildings burned, a whole region
in disorder. That same year, the textile workers of Vera
Cruz state organized secretly the Grand Circle of Free
Workers, the first Mexican labor union. In 1907, they
struck. Again violence, bloodshed, Federal intervention
on behalf of the mills, a lost strike. This affair killed the

Grand Circle. But this syndicalist-anarchist group kept stirring up new strikes—always unsuccessful. This continued until 1911, when Diaz fell.

The importance of the Flores-Magnon brothers to organized labor in Mexico lies in the direction they gave it from the first. In the United States, in Great Britain and to a certain extent in the Continental countries, unionism began in a plain struggle for more favorable hours, conditions and wages. It was more than fifty years before British unionists formed the Labor Party. Even then, the political expression and the trades union expression were organized separately. Not until the C.I.O. arose in 1935 did any large American labor group consciously set out to create a political bloc. And the C.I.O. has not endorsed any revolutionary social theory. But the syndicalist-anarchist idea was implicit in the very charters of the Flores-Magnon unions. Later, international Socialists, our own almost-forgotten I.W.W., and finally Communists, entered Mexico to organize unions committed to the final end of a social revolution.

When, about 1915, Venustiano Carranza came into power as "first chief" and went on to a Presidency which became virtually a dictatorship, Mexican labor had not only attained freedom to organize, but it found unionism encouraged on every hand. In the course of the revolutionary disturbances, politicians and political generals had depended largely on groups of followers organized primarily for purposes other than political. Labor unions constituted ready-made blocs.

So began another tendency which centered around some politician who works for their special interests provided they work for his.

Carranza, in his rise to power, had been playing for support from labor. Owing to his profuse promises, he got it. A demand for a new Federal Constitution was the main plank in his platform. He made good with a Constitution which, in effect, expressed the maximum demands of all the important groups among his followers.

We have already touched on this Constitution of 1917, in so far as it relates to property rights in land and mineral deposits. Further description will help to illuminate those labor politics which so complicated the struggle of the foreign petroleum companies against unstable and ruthless government policies. It is a curious document. Most constitutions, including that of the United States, confine themselves to granting, defining and limiting powers and to stating wide principles. Specific laws to enforce these principles they leave to the legislative branch, on the theory that while principles are eternal, conditions to which they apply change constantly. This one is sprinkled with meticulous ordinances, often applying only to the peculiar conditions of 1917 when the country was going through a social revolution. The long section dealing with the rights and privileges of labor stands as an example. Instead of providing that Congress shall have the power to enact legislation regarding hours and working conditions, it decrees the eight-hour day, makes the provision of free medical service and recreation for employees mandatory on all large employers—and so on. The whole document, especially this part, shows on its face the marks of haste and carelessness.

This was especially true of the Labor Committee of the Constitutional Convention which threw together its part of the document in less than twenty-four hours. Each member, it appeared, asked for his maximum, the rest granted it, and the results went through the ratification virtually without change. But the advanced social legislation which they incorporated—too advanced for Mexico in her state of transition into the industrial age—mostly stood from the first as a dead letter on the statute books. Again with the exception of the petroleum industry. Most of what the Constitutional Convention now demanded by law, the oil companies had given long before.

However, the fact that Mexico had put into her Constitution a bill of rights for labor gave a mighty impetus to organization. The Casa del Obrero Mundial (House of World Labor), to which Carranza had handed the old Jockey Club in Mexico City for headquarters, served as a rallying point during the period of agitation. But the temperamental dictator objected to several strikes designed to make effective the labor articles in the Constitution, and suppressed the Casa. Even before Carranza departed, the unions had begun to amalgamate into the *Confederation Regional Obrera Mexicana,* known for convenience as the C.R.O.M. Under the succeeding administrations, this attained to the place which the American Federation of Labor held in the United States until 1935—the official body. And although its constitution spoke of "The Class Struggle" and "direct action," it was in its working spirit no more radical. However, it did intensify the tendency to make union labor a tool of politics and the rallying point for gangs which supported this or that political leader. Luis Morones, after putting down a Syndicalist named Proal, who had been disturbing the oil district, became its perpetual president. When he became also Minister of Labor in the Obregón cabinet—as though William Green or John L. Lewis, without resigning his present job, should take the seat of Frances Perkins—he perfected the union of politics and organized labor in Mexico. A further refinement of this process was that union organizers found the workers willing to sign up readily enough, but most reluctant to pay their dues. With connivance of the Department of Labor, they proceeded to draw on employees of the federal government for "union funds." So the administration in power was not only chained to the labor unions; it was supporting them indirectly. Although at the height of its power the C.R.O.M. laid claim to 1,500,000 members, a greater proportion of the workers than trades unionism has ever known in the United States, it was a hazy and unstable membership. In the early 1930's even that began to fall away. For one reason because it came out that minor and regional officials were appropriating union funds wholesale to their political or personal uses.

Also, the Mexican labor movement was suddenly becoming radical—not theoretically now, but actually. In spite of Socialist phrases in the Constitution of the C.R.O.M., even its theoretical radicalism had hitherto belonged to the vague North American variety, less concerned with general ideas than with practical results. Ever since Russia went red, Communist agents had operated in Mexico; but for a long time they got little further than they did in the United States. The various administrations had discouraged them; at one time Calles asked our State Department to deport a set of organizers who had slipped across the Rio Grande. But in the late 1920's the Communist International, despairing of any more abrupt and open revolutions, adopted the new policy of the "united front." Its organizers slipped into labor unions, tried to get the controlling offices and, this accomplished, either to lead these followers on by easy stages toward the dictatorship of the proletariat or to throw monkey wrenches into the machinery of capitalism. This worked much better. All this time, a radical rump faction had been holding itself aloof from the C.R.O.M. It began to gain membership.*

As aforesaid, in 1934, Lazaro Cardenas succeeded to the Presidency, virtually by appointment of Calles. Here, the old boss of Mexico made a fatal mistake. Within two years more, this protégé had gone so red that Calles tried to put down the screws on him. In the hidden conflict that ensued, Cardenas won and Calles went into exile as a "dangerous citizen."

Cardenas is a curious figure in whose blood and sentiments the Indian predominates. He has that personal courage of body and mind so much esteemed in Mexico; but it is imperfectly balanced by judgment. In a series of speeches and manifestos, he seemed to announce the intention of adopting the whole leftist program. And he proceeded with that six-year plan on the apparent assumption that material and social improvement could be attained by confiscation of private property.

Under him organized labor began to gather about a new and redder focus. The Confederation of Mexican Labor (known as the C.T.M.), a small, independent body in the days when Morones flourished, came suddenly into the foreground. With it arose another man who has set his peculiar stamp on all Mexican politics. Vicente Lombardo Toledano is a mestizo who began his career as a university professor. Radical from the first, his opinions, his contentiousness or his constant agitation—per-

---

*For much of the material embodied in the early part of this chapter, we are indebted to Marjorie Ruth Clark's *Organized Labor in Mexico,* the standard work on that subject in English.

haps all three—cost him his university job. He drifted further and further toward communism. No one knows whether he belongs actually to that party, but at least, like the Dutch cook in *Davy and the Goblin,* he behaves as such. Of late years he has visited Russia where he established cordial relations with Stalin. On his way home, he stopped in the United States long enough to make several fiery speeches endorsing the dictatorship of the proletariat. From the beginning of the Cardenas administration, the government seems to have recognized him as the "labor chief." Then, in 1935, a period when things began to happen all at once, he delivered in Mexico City a series of so-called lectures—in reality revolutionary harangues. Enthusiasm and distaste for Toledano swelled until it burst in a gory riot at the center of Mexico City—an affair which amounted to a pitched battle. It is significant that the newspapers, in reporting this affair, called Toledano's opposition indifferently and interchangeably the "C.R.O.M." and "followers of Calles," so expressing the inseparable bond between politics and organized labor in contemporary Mexico. The Toledanistas won handily. When the ambulances departed, Toledano had control of the C.T.M. And Cardenas, to all practical purposes, had control of Toledano. They have worked together, although perhaps not with uninterrupted harmony, ever since. For power and importance, Toledano was by 1937 the republic's second citizen.

From the moment when Cardenas assumed office and announced his ultra-revolutionary program, the oil companies about Tampico—the distinctly American district as the area south of Vera Cruz is the Dutch and British —began to have constant, irritating employee-trouble. It seemed to rain agitators and politicians eager to establish cordial relations with the exigent labor leaders. Labor in the industry had been organized long before— indeed, the Petroleum Workers' Union had virtually established a closed shop. In 1934, President Rodriguez, immediate predecessor of Cardenas, had intervened in a dispute between a petroleum company and its labor to write into the contract a provision known popularly as the "Exclusion Clause." Its main provisions are about as follows: The company cannot hire any man for any position usually covered by labor contracts unless he belongs to a labor union. No man may be discharged by the company without payment of a very heavy indemnity. The union, however, has the right to demand and to effect the discharge of any of its members without stating its reasons for the demand. This meant, of course, that the expelled member was permanently out of a job in the petroleum industry. Cardenas extended this principle to other industries and made it in effect the law of the land. The typical Mexican labor union of today not only works hand in glove with the government but imitates the government in being a dictatorship under deceptively democratic forms. Usually, the leaders not only form all policies but make all smaller decisions; getting a member expelled is for them as easy as lying. This constitutes a terrible penalty against the dissenter, especially since a reputation for having been expelled from the Petroleum Workers as a disturber might follow him in case he tried to get a job in other industries. From the time when the "Exclusion Clause" became effective, one indiscreet word of criticism, one act of disobedience toward his leader, might ruin life for any mere dues-payer.

Early in the shift of Mexican labor toward the left, the Petroleum Workers' Union joined hands with the

C.T.M. The high wages in the petroleum industry, the unique services furnished free by the companies—schools, scholarships, technical training, modern housing, sanitation, medical care, pensions, savings funds—did not prevent these new leaders from springing a series of strikes, sometimes over trivial incidents, sometimes over wage-scales. Mexico has a Federal Labor Board with considerably wider powers than our own. At first the companies appealed to this tribunal. Almost invariably it decided in favor of the unions. No more appeals! Then in some branches of the industry, the leaders began applying an especially irritating form of sabotage. They ordered the workers on all jobs not listed as routine to slow down their former pace by eighty to eighty-five per cent. This, they explained blandly, made more work. Also, there were storm signs from the government quarter. One was a set of regulations plainly designed to supplant the experienced, highly educated American management with Mexicans. Men chosen by the unions were to receive two years of intensive education in the higher processes of extracting and refining oil; after which, they were to jump into executive jobs. In modern days, an American who rises to the top in the technical branches of the petroleum business has usually behind him at least a decade of special education. The unions, which meant the politicians, were to choose these future general managers, superintendents of refineries, chemical experts. Well, there was once a parallel situation in Russia. "Big Bill" Haywood, old leader of the Western Federation of Miners, having fled from the United States to avoid a jail sentence, created so much enthusiasm among the Communists that they made him director of mines for the whole Soviet Republic. He knew a great deal about labor unions; but all he knew about managing mines he had picked up as a driller in the drifts. And it worked out unfortunately for both Russia and Big Bill. But the petroleum companies swallowed all this, as they swallowed many another hampering imposition. They had to.

Clouds were gathered from the outside. Now, Cardenas seemed to be trying to drive foreign capital out of the country, no matter what the cost to Mexico or the injustice to the investor. He had eliminated the last foreign interest in the main Mexican railroads, had turned them over to the railroad unions and, when that did not work, nationalized them. With the usual airy promise to pay at some future time, he had grabbed the important cotton fields of the north-central district. Here foreign owners, British and American, had broken the land, introduced modern methods, made Mexico nearly independent of imports for her important cotton textile industry. Out they went; and the land, in small tracts, was divided among former laborers who might or might not know anything about cotton-growing except how to plant and pick it. Toward the end of 1935 President Cardenas made a speech which, we know now, was his first pass at the oil industry. "We expect the capitalist class," he said in substance, "to pay labor up to the limit of its economic capacity." That last phrase, which, literally interpreted, meant that business must run without any expectation of profit, passed almost unnoticed at the time. Cardenas was speaking to a labor audience, and Mexican politicians, even more than those of less radical lands, have a way of promising more on the platform than they perform in their offices. Optimists among the American and British oil men still maintained that, in view of his past experience with the economic collapse of state-conducted enterprises, Cardenas could not be so reckless as vitally to disturb a business which was paying nearly 60,000,000 pesos a year in direct and indirect taxes. But when he laid down the same principle in a message to Congress, even the optimists began to take apprehensive notice.

We never know our luck. At about this time, a British company, working at Poza Rica in the southern district, made its sensational discoveries on land which it had long owned. After the political blight fell on the industry, Mexican oil production had declined steadily to 32,000,000 barrels in the early 1930's. The Poza Rica wells raised the figures to 46,000,000 barrels; and prospects for further increase seemed bright. One cannot look into the minds of President Cardenas and his advisors. It seems probable, however, that this gust of new prosperity brought the psychological turning point in the relations between the Mexican government and the petroleum industry. With higher production in sight Cardenas might by seizing and nationalizing the wells make them return revenues higher than mere taxes; and the government was in desperate need of more money. Of course, Great Britain and Holland would protest and the United States would demand "prompt, assured and effectual payment" for the expropriated property of their nationals. They had done that when Obregón began grabbing the large landed estates, and they had made trouble over the seizure of foreign capital invested in the railroads. But Mexico had managed to evade payment and could doubtless do it again. This time, however, he must sugar a morally indefensible act with a coating of false legal justification.

The operation began in the early summer of 1936. All the companies had contracts with their workers regarding wages, hours and conditions. Suddenly the executives of the Petroleum Workers' Union went into a huddle which lasted for months. The meeting was so long and so melodramatically secret as to attract attention and cause gossip. The companies learned from indirect sources that the union leaders were thrashing out a new, uniform and drastic general agreement with which they intended arbitrarily to replace all existing contracts. Calmly but apprehensively, the executives waited and worked until November 3rd. On that day, the ordinary mails brought a huge envelope to nearly every general manager in the Mexican field. It contained a letter of enclosure which amounted to an ultimatum. The union had noted "the discontent of the petroleum workers and the existing lack of economic equilibrium due exclusively to the diversity of working conditions obtaining in the industry." Enclosed the recipient would find a new and uniform contract to govern the relations of the companies with their labor in the Mexican oil fields. It must supersede all existing contracts, no matter how long they had to run. If all of the companies so notified had not signed it without alteration within ten days, the Petroleum Workers' Union would promptly call on the eleventh day a general strike.

The contract covered 165 foolscap-size pages. If any American employer had received through the mails such a document as this proved to be, he would have probably taken it for an elaborate practical joke. But the foreign oil men had long lived in an atmosphere where the fantastic is the commonplace. Here are the chief final demands of the Petroleum Workers' Union, most of which were set down in this "model contract."

A forty-hour week with fifty-six-hour pay.

A horizontal increase in wages all up and down the line. Some of these increases ran as high as thirty-five per cent. The minimum demand was seven pesos a day for un-skilled laborers, as a basic wage alone.

In case the companies reduced personnel, the men laid off must receive ninety days' pay, plus twenty-five days for each year of service. The companies might not shift personnel from one job to another without the consent of the union.

The companies must furnish free medical, surgical and dental service regardless of the origin or cause of the illness. This must apply not only to employees but to their families. What constituted a family was most carefully defined—the worker's wife, children, parents, grand-parents, great-grandparents, grandchildren and brothers and sisters under sixteen years of age.

When a company erected housing for its workers it must allow the union to select the site. Further, the housing must be built from plans furnished or approved by the union.

The companies, again at their own sole expense, must provide and maintain offices, meeting halls and clerical staffs for the exclusive use of the unions in their respective territories. They must provide cars and chauffeurs, with upkeep and wages, for the exclusive use of the union leaders.

Whenever a delegate went to a union convention, the company for which he worked must pay him his regular wages, no matter how long he might linger; also it must furnish him first-class railway transportation. The contract set no limit to the numbers of such delegates.

Already, the law provided that a company which lost a strike by award of the Labor Board must pay the workers for the time lost in striking. This contract demanded full pay for the term of every strike, no matter which side won.

The companies must furnish overalls, and also provide laundry service for all working clothes.

The section regarding vacations and holidays began with the fundamental demand that every employee who had been in service of a company for from one day to five years should have a yearly vacation of twenty-one working days—intervening Saturdays, Sundays and holidays not counting. Five to ten years of service called for forty days; ten to fifteen years, sixty days; all this with full pay.

The company, on demand, must furnish any worker going on vacation with first-class transportation to and from any point which he chose to visit.

At any time, and as often as desired, any workman might have, on request, three days' leave of absence with full pay.

On a long visit of holidays, civic and religious, there was to be no work—but full pay.

The contract demanded heavy extra pay for overtime. If a weekly rest day (Saturday or Sunday), an "obligatory rest day" and a holiday fell on the same date, any man who worked would receive four times his normal pay.

For work at certain heights normal to operations in oil refineries, for work at certain temperatures, the men must receive three times their usual pay. Any man ordered to work out of doors when it was raining must receive double his usual pay.

This singular document came to a climax in the clauses regarding management.

They began with the flat demand that the company might not reduce personnel nor discharge any employee without full consent and approval of the syndicate; nor might any employee in refineries, terminals and main offices be moved, transferred or relocated without the approval of that same court of last resort. The contract then moved on up to the offices, where a certain proportion of executives, such as superintendents and heads of sub-departments, must be members of the union and responsible for their actions to the union alone. These positions were all specified. They amounted to about half of the executive forces.

These are just some of the highlights. But perhaps the reader who does not know his Mexico may need some enlightenment on a few special points in this unique document. First, the matter of wages—here let us go back to the conditions before the unions made this amazing demand. Always the oil business had not only paid its help, from top to bottom, better than any other industry in Mexico, but almost fantastically higher than the average. Mexican government statistics, most certainly not rigged in favor of the oil companies, alone prove that. In the report for 1936, the contrast stood as follows:

Average Wages (in Pesos)	Daily	Annual
PETROLEUM	7.42	2,671.20
Light and Power	5.09	1,832.40
Street Railways	4.55	1,638.00
Mining	4.32	1,555.20
Textiles	3.13	1,126.80

A better comparison, however, appears when one considers the daily wages as classified by crafts. These, on the same authority, were:

Daily Wages (in Pesos)	Petroleum	Average of all Mex. Industries
Masons	5.20 to 8.40	1.89
Carpenters	4.00 to 8.40	2.05
Chauffeurs	4.80 to 6.00	2.26
Electricians	6.00 to 7.60	2.74
Stevedores	3.00	2.05
Blacksmiths	7.25	1.98
Unskilled Labor	3.00 to 3.50	1.13

In the schedule presented with the demands of the union, the various crafts engaged in the petroleum industry were so classified as to make complete detailed comparison with the government statistics on other industries rather difficult. But to give two obvious examples, unskilled laborers were set down in the proposed contract for a minimum of seven pesos a day and chauffeurs for twenty pesos a day.

That is not the full story. After the government gathered the figures for this report of 1936, the petroleum companies, to meet an increase in the cost of living, had raised the entire wage scale about twenty-six per cent. Further, almost alone among Mexican industries they furnished free housing, free medical care, with hospitalization when necessary, for the workers and their wives and children; scholarships, good schools, playgrounds and sport equipment. Company accountants calculated that these social benefits increased the basic wage by about ninety per cent. Making liberal allowance for certain benefits which not every worker used, it seems fair to say that the actual wage in the petroleum industry was at least fifty per cent higher than the government estimates, which dealt only with direct cash payments. Therefore, the real average daily earning was eleven or twelve pesos a day instead of 7.42, as stated in the estimates of the government.

The absurdities of the provisions regarding union delegates and union headquarters require no comment.

Already the companies were granting holidays of from seven to fourteen days a year, according to the local customs of the districts in which they worked. Also, they were giving vacations running up to eighteen days a year, according to the length of service. A rough computation showed that under the proposed contract the average working year would amount to about 223 days—with pay for 365. This was the maximum. No one could be quite sure how many men would use their "three days' leave of absence on full pay" to lead a life of elegant idleness blurred only by a call at the office every third day in order to apply for a new lease of leisure. No one could tell how often the union might call a strike in order to give the men a vacation on full pay. Just so, in computing costs they could not tell how many among their forces would develop an itch for the broadening influence of travel and, when vacation time neared, demand first-class passage to and from Niagara Falls, Yellowstone Park, Hollywood, Paris, the Riviera or Russia.

As for the "grandmother clause" regarding medical benefits, that too was an uncertain quantity. Mexicans have large families. The doctors and hospitals might expect a rush of parents, grandparents and brothers and sisters under sixteen. To sum it all up, company statisticians, working accurately on the certain factors such as the demands for increased wages and shorter hours and estimating the uncertain, calculated that this proposed contract might raise their labor costs by 300,000,000 pesos a year. That was about as much annually as the net profit of all the companies for the last ten years! Cardenas had laid down the principle that business must pay wages "to the limit of economic capacity." These demands went far beyond that limit.

Yet the most troublesome demon sitting on the pillow of every American, Dutch and British executive on the night of November 3, 1936, was the long passage dealing with "superior and confidential employees." There the proposed contract was very specific. It named the offices and positions. Nearly every assistant to a general manager, department manager, sales manager or superintendent must be a member of the union, selected by the union. In many cases, the executives could guess at the identity of the new assistants. Some of them would be incompetents who owed their promotion to prominence in the union or—what amounts to the same thing in modern Mexico—political pull. It would be the Big Bill Haywood story all over again. Others, indeed, would be old employees who had proved themselves inherently competent. But even these men would be primarily responsible to the union, not to the company. Over their heads would hang by a thread the axe of the "Exclusion Clause." If they disobeyed orders from the union leader or from the Cardenas machine, the union might expel them; which would mean virtually permanent unemployment. The politicians and the union leaders would know all the trade secrets of all the oil companies. They could disturb and clog production whenever their fancy dictated. They could—oh, but what was the use? In such a situation, no business could carry on for a month.

Ever since Toledano made himself master of Mexican labor, executives of the oil companies had been suspecting that the Federal government was out to grab the petroleum industry; and the events of the year ending in November, 1936, had turned this belief almost into a certainty. Most of them, as they finished reading the union manifesto, thought, "this is the beginning of the end." They had not expected that the first wave of attack would strike at this point; but they had no doubt whatever that the objective was nationalization of the oil companies—and of course, without any real compensation. The Mexican Federal government, in the course of subsequent events, blandly denied that the demands of the union had any relation to the issue of public ownership. But in 1938, after Mexico had seized the properties, Toledano let at least the head of the cat out of the bag. On his way back from a visit to the radical labor leaders in Europe, he stopped in New York to deliver one of his rousing incendiary speeches. He reviewed the whole story of the oil confiscations in Mexico from the ultra-radical position. When he came to a point—somewhat in advance of this narrative—where the companies offered to raise wages to the tune of 26,000,000 pesos a year, he paused and added impressively:

> This offer Cardenas refused. If we had accepted, it would have been a victory of labor over capital within the Mexican oil industry; but by refusing the offer, we won a great victory for the Mexican people against foreign imperialism.

Which, translated not only from Spanish into English but from oratory into plain language, means that Cardenas and Toledano were out for confiscation from the beginning, and that the demands of the union were never the real issue but merely the opening gun in the campaign. They were impossible, of course.

The reckless course that Cardenas was steering ran past two dangerous reefs—foreign antagonism and public opinion. As soon as he seized all petroleum properties he might expect to hear from the British and Dutch foreign offices and the American State Department. Any dictator, even one who seems to sit as firmly in his saddle as Adolf Hitler, must reckon with public opinion—else he would not go to the expense and trouble of maintaining domestic propaganda. In Mexico, powerful and intelligent elements, not all of them conservative, remembered the futile performances of the old government-controlled oil company and feared the effects of expropriation. From the bankers to the corner grocers, business would probably stand solidly against this policy. Probably also, even the majority of the petroleum workers looked upon it with emotions ranging from distaste to horror. Their high wages and their special working conditions had made them the aristocracy of Mexican labor. They remembered that the bankrupt government-owned company paid wages barely above the subsistence level, on the plea that Mexicans must suffer for a time in order to help create the workingman's paradise. And at that, it had shown itself incompetent to find oil for itself. But they were between the devil and the deep sea. The union leaders, with the guns of the government behind them, could by means of the "Exclusion Clause" not only throw any dissenter out of work but probably keep him out of work for life. The Mexican has a talent for silence; and in all this controversy no one has ever known what the rank-and-file of the workers thought about it.

The actions of Cardenas during the next few months reveal his thoughts and intentions. This contract, embracing terms which no sane business man could be expected to accept, furnished a pretext for dragging the case before the courts, the Labor Board and a half dozen other tribunals. In the subsequent hearings and "investigations" he could pack the record with vague charges, plain falsehoods and half-truths all aiming at the same conclusion —that the foreign oil companies were parasites, sucking the blood of Mexico and oppressing Mexican labor. He had by now an incomplete but quite satisfactory control over national journalism. The newspapers, generally speaking, would present to the public only the governmental version of the story. With the help of Toledano, agitating through the C.T.M., he could lash up in labor such a hatred of "foreign oppressors" as to abate all fear of revolution when he came to the decisive act.

Further, by this process he might present to the Mexican public an appearance of moral justification when the American, British and Dutch governments made the inevitable protests or asked for spot cash in payment. At the end, he must encounter an awkward problem. Repeatedly, the Mexican Supreme Court had ruled that any land rights or subsoil rights legally acquired before May 1, 1917, constituted private property and, if expropriated, must be paid for on the dot. That principle, indeed, was written into the Constitution. Well, there were ways to handle that also. The way he chose will presently appear.

Now we return to the managers of the oil companies. Hopeless as the case looked, they intended of course to fight. Men of their stripe do not meekly abandon hundreds of millions of dollars' worth of property and work to which they have given the best years of their lives. By argument and diplomacy, they persuaded the union to extend the ultimatum for two weeks. There, the labor leaders stood pat. Unless by November 27th the companies had agreed to sign the contract as written, the order for a general strike would go into effect at once.

Then, just before the deadline, President Cardenas for the first time appeared openly in the affair. He proposed a convention "to conclude, within a period of six months at the most, a collective contract to be made obligatory." Presumably, obligatory on the companies alone. On the day set for the strike, the companies and the union signed the agreement establishing the convention—really, a conference between representatives of the company and of the union with an official of the Department of Labor. Already Cardenas had hung a sword by a hair over the heads of the companies. On November 3, 1936—the day when the unions presented their first demands and also the day of the American presidential elections—the Mexican Congress remained in permanent session. That night, it gave Cardenas the power to expropriate by decree the property of the foreign-owned petroleum companies.

The conference lasted for nearly six months of intermittent wrangling. The union not only fought every step of the way, but kept adding to its terms—as when it demanded that all the Mexican workers on the oil tankers be added to the Petroleum Workers and benefit by the new contract. An attempt to argue it out clause by clause dragged the discussions out to May 1, 1937, and got no one anywhere. The companies asked for a ten-day recess, at the end of which they submitted their terms.

First, they offered to divide "confidential positions" into four classes, with union representation so arranged therein that no labor leader could tie up production. At that, this concession would have increased greatly the number of union men in the executive forces.

They agreed that whenever they reduced personnel, they would give their reasons to the union. Procedure in cases of discharge was to follow the terms laid down in the Federal Labor Law.

When they reduced personnel, they would give the men so laid off three months' pay plus an allowance of twenty days for each year of service with the company.

As to the clause in the proposed contract forbidding the companies to move personnel without consent of the union, they yielded this right in the case of employees in the refineries, the terminals and the general offices. They would reserve the right to themselves in the case of men employed in camps and in the sales department.

They agreed to pension all workers who had completed twenty to twenty-five years of service.

They reserved to themselves the right to determine the sites, the material and the plans for all housing.

They were willing to discuss the question of longer vacation periods.

They would continue to give the workers free medical service, free medicines, the care of specialists in certain cases. This applied also to wives and children, but not to the horde of relations mentioned in the union contract. In cases of temporary incapacity due to accidents while at work or other occupational causes, they would pay full wages. In other types of injury or illness, besides medical care, they would grant certain payments for lost time.

In certain cases, such as permanent disability through industrial accidents, they would pay pensions running up to seventy-five per cent of the victim's wages before the accident.

They would grant seven "obligatory holidays" and seven and a half "extra holidays" each year on full pay.

They agreed to give every permanent worker who had been employed for a year or more an annual vacation of eighteen days a year. Temporary workers were to enjoy the same privilege after any year in which they had worked for 275 days.

They refused to furnish and pay permanent office staffs for the union locals or cars with chauffeurs for their leaders. They did agree to furnish headquarters for each local, with such necessary services as water and light.

And they would raise wages by about 13,000,000 pesos a year.

The union's reply was to throw the proposal back into the face of the management. It refused to alter the proposed contract by so much as an adjective. Promptly, it called the long-expected, long-dreaded general strike. By May 28th, the petroleum business, second largest single commercial asset of Mexico, had stopped dead.

Two days after the strike began, another federal agency came into the picture—the Labor Board. This bureau, very important to the rest of this story, must be carefully distinguished from the Department of Labor which has much the same power and jurisdiction as our own.

Its full legal title is the Federal Board of Mediation and Arbitration and it has complex and curious functions. It must pass on the legality of every strike. This means that it determines whether a majority of the workers involved demand new conditions and whether the parties to the contract have complied with the law in such routine matters as notification. It has not the right to intervene, on its own initiative. But on request of one of the parties involved, it may arbitrate any strike.

Its record, from the viewpoint of the companies, was such as to create apprehension. Up to this time, it had ruled as court of last resort on about 900 labor disputes, and more than ninety-six per cent of its decisions had gone in favor of the workers. It declared now that a "state of strike existed" in the petroleum industry. After this declaration, it might find means to intervene under Article 260, Section I of the Federal Labor Law—especially if the union demanded arbitration. The attorneys for the oil companies, who feared no tribunal more than this one, challenged the order in the courts, asserting that the peculiar conditions of this strike made that law inapplicable.

Then suddenly President Cardenas intervened again. He had his reasons. Public opinion is usually the determining factor in any strike. And this one was not popular, probably even with most of the strikers. In the circumstances, a vote among the petroleum workers no more expressed real opinion than a Nazi plebiscite. Since Cardenas had not openly endorsed the action of the Petroleum Workers' Union, the newspapers felt free to criticize it—and generally did. Already it was casting a blight on business in all central Mexico. Cardenas asked the gentlemen of the union and the gentlemen of the foreign oil companies to give him their best terms. The union stood pat. The companies added other concessions —offered to raise the minimum wage set down in their counter-proposal and to increase several other social and economic benefits. But they made this new proposition conditional upon unmodified acceptance of the counter-proposal and the immediate signature of a contract. Again the union refused flatly. The strike went on. It grew more and more unpopular.

Then somebody in the union or the government found a way. Mexican laws differ so widely from those of the United States that fully to explain the next move would weary the reader without instructing him. It is enough to say that the Federal Labor Law gives the Labor Board the power to intervene and investigate whenever a strike involves "causes of an economic order . . . which cannot by their *special nature* be determined in the ordinary manner." After the strike had gone on for more than a week and both the workers and the public had begun to feel its hardships, the union suddenly made an appeal to the Labor Board based on this provision of law. It asked that the Board investigate fully the financial condition of the companies and compel them to grant not only all the demands in the proposed contract presented on November 3rd, but those added in the course of the long negotiations—and all this without prejudice of the union's right to receive the 13,000,000 pesos a year in increased salaries which the companies had offered as a compromise. That concession, the union added, had been forced through "strike pressure."

The Board, by a majority vote, granted the petition and took charge. More to the point at the moment, it ordered the strike suspended during the period of the investigation, thereby getting President Cardenas out of a bad hole. On June 9, 1937, the men went back to their jobs.

All set now—going in the direction that the pessimists had prophesied, even though the route was a little un-expected. The labor leaders knew, of course, that no company could stay in business or even produce oil very long on such terms as they proposed. They were playing for higher stakes than victory in a mere strike. From this time forth, events moved, irregularly but on the whole steadily, toward nationalization of the industry. The separate maneuvers seem odd, sometimes blind, often tragically comic. But now that the affair is over, the details fit into an exceptionally neat pattern.

CHAPTER IV

The Seizure of the Oil Industry

T HAT APPEAL to the Labor Board set the stage for
the final act. To one unacquainted with the mental
cast of the Mexican people, the spirit and origins
of Mexican law and the singular position of President
Cardenas, those legal proceedings which marked the
years 1937 and 1938, told baldly, would in spots seem
inexplicable. Let us begin, then, with a few paragraphs
of explanation and clarification. None in recent years has
stated more succinctly those peculiar, contradictory
characteristics of the Mexican mind which bear on the
present controversy than John Serocold, an Englishman
with long experience in the country. The secret of Mexican psychology, he writes:

> Must be sought on the shores of the Pacific. Scholars have
> yet to define, and geographers to explain, the resemblance
> between the art of the Chou dynasty in China and that of the
> Aztecs and Mayas. Even today the mental processes of the
> Chinese and the central American Indians, though highly
> different in their results, resemble one another in the way
> action is determined and cultural forms are developed, not
> by reasoning upward from a premise or an analysis but simply
> by the lateral addition of experience as it comes.

> The Mexican Indian has a gentle sensitive nature and he is
> abnormally sensitive to, and disturbed by, any form of logical

insistence on those absolute values, spiritual, legal and material, which obtain among other peoples and constitute the basis of their public and private intercourse. But his gentleness is apathetic; he does not care, as we do, to practice the restraint of his impulses; let a convention be his inheritance, or an idea take hold of him, and he will follow it to the last, at the cost of his prosperity, his word, and if necessary his life. His motives are incalculable and his behavior, though based on those motives, cannot be adduced to them by any train of logic. Thus, in our parlance, he is the victim of double unreason and that is why relations between him and foreigners are so often unsatisfactory. It is not so much that the arguments of the two collide. They do not meet at all . . .

This is not to deny the existence or practical capacity of those many intelligent and patriotic Mexicans who have given and are giving their best energies to the country's well-being. The Indian character may be their inspiration but it is also their difficulty. They partake of it emotionally. Their task is to reconcile it in their policies with the forces of the modern world.

And upon that singular mentality, Mexico has built further strangeness, by her peculiar state system of education. As we have already shown, when Diaz fell less than twenty per cent of the populace was literate. Among the rising generation, illiteracy has shrunk to less than fifty per cent. The schools which have done this work are state-supported and the plaything of politics. Just as in contemporary Germany the Nazis hammer their peculiar racial and political theories into the juvenile head, just as in Communist Russia all teaching from the kindergarten to the higher degrees rests on the Marxian doctrine of economics, so in Mexico all public education has for the past quarter of a century based itself upon the idea of a revolution—a popular movement, its objectives and principles defined in a manner which seems, to the Western European mind, somewhat vague and contradictory. The practical result is a psychology fascinated with change for the sake of change, accepting as axioms those political excesses, illogical proceedings and short-cuts which mark all revolutions.

Indeed, that revolutionary psychology, together with the mental habit of reasoning "by the lateral addition of experience," does much to account for the curious Mexican Constitution with its jumble of eternal principles and temporary ordinances, its occasional contradictions. The laws built upon this foundation, and especially those regarding labor, have the same characteristics. Successive revolutionary administrations have met temporary emergencies by piling up special laws with little or no regard for the interests of the commonwealth as a whole, or, indeed, for the ultimate good of labor. Some are unenforceable; and some, like those requiring employers to give their workers such social benefits as housing and medical care, seem to be enforced only against foreigners.

Finally, one must remember, in explaining the actions of President Cardenas himself, a special factor which influences all dictatorships be they ancient or modern. The Roman Emperor had his praetorian guard; Hitler has his brownshirts, Stalin his Communist Party and his secret police. Nominally, the leader dictates to them and they are only his agents in dictating to the populace. Really, their composite opinion and common interests influence his actions—sometimes even control them. The Mexican dictatorship is of course not so strong and potent as the German, the Italian or the Russian. But it follows the same laws. Under Cardenas, the labor leaders and labor politicians form this praetorian guard. Even if these men were not radical at heart, the political necessity for distributing apparent largesse to their followers would drive them on to constantly larger and more greedy demands for expropriation. In the first four years of his administration, Cardenas seized and distributed or nationalized more land, more industrial establishments and public utilities and more fundamental resources in general than all of his predecessors put together. It is possible that even he, reckless and hasty of judgment though he may be, saw at moments the dangers in this over-rapid process of putting vast national resources into the hands of ex-peons with no tradition of personal property and no skill in using it. So too, in this matter of the foreign oil companies, perhaps Cardenas shrank at times from the implications of the arbitrary policy he was following. During the vital year 1937, there were curious pauses in the drive against the petroleum companies, as though someone in high authority had delayed matters in the hope that an unforeseen event might make further progress in this direction impossible. Then would come a burst of pressure from the rear, and affairs would move along their bizarre course toward the end which the radical labor leaders desired.

Whatever lawyer conceived the idea of appealing the union's case to the Labor Board on the grounds of an "economic issue" deserves credit for his ingenuity. When, in 1931, Congress passed the revised labor laws, almost invariably favorable to the workers, it inserted one clause for protection of the employers. A union might strike for terms which the Labor Board, called in to mediate, considered just. But granting these terms might make it impossible for a financially embarrassed company to continue in business. So the employer might appeal on "economic grounds" and present witnesses and accounts to prove its case. The Board, if it found the contention good, might then adjust hours, wages and conditions in such a manner as to avert bankruptcy from the employer and consequent unemployment from the workers.

Blocked by the unpopularity of their recent strike, the labor leaders looked about for some other weapon by which to achieve the nationalization of the oil industry. They found it in the "economic issue," which they now turned away from its original purpose and used for their own ends in an appeal to the Labor Board. They had one reason for doing this, and one alone. A proceeding of this nature, in contrast with regular arbitration proceedings, would involve examination of the employer's books and accounts. It was within the letter of the law, probably, but it so plainly violated the spirit and intent of the law that company attorneys believed they might beat it by an appeal to the courts. However, they had appealed once before; and this time, refusal to appear would give the opposition grounds for declaring that they were afraid to show their books. Nevertheless, they quite understood the motives behind the transaction. Toledano had been lashing up anti-foreign sentiment. Already he was shouting from the platform such phrases as "financial imperialism" and "Colossus of the North." Cardenas had been hinting, other politicians had been declaring openly, that the companies were making fantastic profits, which went into the pockets of "greedy foreigners." The unions or the government—which by now came to the same thing—could juggle the accounts to make the charge of swollen profits appear true and sound. Yet the companies decided to fight on that line. It seemed the only thing to do.

The Labor Board, however, professed that it needed fuller information and enlightenment. It appointed, therefore, a "commission of experts" to hold hearings, make investigations, examine the finances of the petroleum companies and within six months render a full report which, the Board seemed to hint, would receive the official blessing. Three men composed the commission proper. Two of them were officials in the financial departments of the government, and may be dismissed as unimportant to the story. The third, who occupied the position of its secretary-general, was Jesus Silva Herzog, investigator for the Department of National Economy. He, like Toledano, was a university professor grown great in radical politics. He was an avowed Communist. It was plain from the first that he would do most of the work, make the important decisions, direct the investigation and either write the report or edit the contents to express his own views.

Both sides were allowed the services of experts. The unions chose either men from their own ranks or lawyers and accountants identified with the labor movement. The companies named the following men—all Mexican citizens and only two or three in any way connected with the petroleum industry:

Rafael Mancera, formerly Assistant Secretary of the Treasury; now an eminent and reputable certified public accountant.

Roberto Cases Alatriske, an auditor of the Bank of Mexico.

Ingeniero Ezequiel Ordoñez, a past director of the National Institute of Geology, called by his countrymen "the father of oil production in Mexico."

Ingeniero Joaquin Santaella, economist and engineer, holder of high positions in the Mexican government.,

Dr. Gustavo Baz, prominent surgeon of Mexico City.

Dr. Fernando Ocaranza, author, once rector of the National University.

Mario Dominguez, head of one of the leading savings banks and actuary of the largest life insurance company in Mexico.

Emilio Velarde, actuary.

In addition, the companies assigned men in their own employ, each experienced in such phases of oil business as accountancy, labor relations, production and shipping, to advise their representatives on the committee.

So the Commission and the experts for both sides settled down to a proceeding which violated from the first the principles of abstract justice held in any land. It was as though a judge haled the accused into court, arraigned him, pronounced him guilty, sentenced him to death and then proceeded in a long-drawn-out trial to attempt to justify the decision. The only parallel in modern times is one of those Russian "purge" trials where the judge says to the accused, "You are not here to defend your acts; you are here to confess your guilt and receive sentence of death."

It began with a long questionnaire submitted to the oil companies—a most thorough inquiry into every phase of their business. Of course, in addition to this, accountants for the unions were going through the books and others of their experts were making a close inspection of the plants. Almost at once, the companies perceived that the inquiry was taking a course hostile to their legitimate interests. All of the union experts were limiting their questions to the three years between 1934 and 1936 inclusive, and that was decidedly unfair. Extraction of petroleum is only a form of mining; and as such, a hazardous and speculative business. The industry has its good and bad years, often independently of good and bad times in general business. It depends largely on the good luck of striking a rich deposit or the bad luck of striking nothing at all. In the case of the Mexican petroleum companies, conditions imposed by the government had made exploration for new deposits, as a business venture, either impossible or extremely risky. Laws or the unfair administration of laws prevented them from acquiring and opening up new fields in areas where geology had proved the probable existence of petroleum deposits; and ordinary commercial prudence had restrained them from expending millions in exploring lands which they already owned—the future seemed far too uncertain. But a British company had taken a chance on its own land and opened up the Poza Rica district with a gush of oil which exceeded all expectations. Production had been declining steadily since 1921; now it rose by a few million barrels a year. Generally speaking, only the company which made the Poza Rica discovery enjoyed these benefits, but for two or three years they gave to the whole industry an appearance of comparative prosperity. Even these conditions were only temporary. Soon the Poza Rica borings would finish their phenomenal first flow and become just another set of good oil wells, while the European governments, then heavy buyers of gasoline for their new armaments, would either finish stocking up or begin to supply themselves from the phenomenal new deposits just opened in the Far East. Then the business in Mexico, prevented as it was from any expansion, would decline again to the point where many of the companies went into the red. A fair basis for estimating profits, the companies believed, would be the ten-year period ending in 1937. They expressed this view, officially, to Professor Herzog.

He did not deign to answer.

Another unfair line of investigation appeared in both the questionnaire and the private inquiries of the union experts. They wanted to know all about wages and conditions in the oil industry of the United States. Evidently they intended to jack up wages to the scale paid north of the Rio Grande. Of course, both the standard and the cost of living are widely different in Mexico and the United States; this and other considerations would make the comparison valueless, except for the purpose of propaganda.

Again the companies protested; and again the commission, as represented by Herzog, made no reply. So the inquiry went on for weeks, through constant haggling, constant snubbing of the companies and their representatives. Suddenly, Herzog closed the inquiry and started to prepare his report. Just thirty days later he gave it out. It was 900,000 words long. That meant an output of 30,000 words a day, Sundays included. The reader may be unaccustomed to thinking of "copy" in terms of "wordage." Be it known, therefore, that an average magazine article comprises about 4,000 words and that 900,000 words exceeds the length of *Gone with the Wind*. Some of the Mexican newspapers defied the visible and invisible censorship to comment ironically on Professor Herzog's extraordinary fecundity and to hint that the bulk of this document predated even the strike in the oil fields. It began with a long, scholarly history of Mexican petroleum in the prehistoric and Inca periods. When it reached modern times it read like the opening address of a prosecuting attorney. It railed against the companies; it blasted them with hot Spanish adjectives; it strayed both from the subject in hand and from the researches of the committee to make absurd charges for which it offered no pretence of proof; and it ended with a proposed labor contract. This last, by the way, was an added starter. The terms did not differ greatly from the original demands of the unions. It shaved down a few of the union's proposed wage schedules, but in other respects it added new and most awkward conditions. However, the important and interesting feature was the chapter dealing with the finances of the petroleum companies, all bearing on their "capacity to pay."

To state the matter in brief, Professor Herzog and associates found that the companies had at the end of 1936, reserves and surplus of 77,185,946 pesos; and that in the 1934–1936 period they returned an average net profit of 16.81 per cent on their invested capital.

As a matter of fact, the eminent neutral auditors who went over the books of the companies found that the cash reserves and surplus were about 26,000,000 pesos and the profits in the 1934–1936 period were 7.5 per cent. That does not tell the whole story—the "commission of experts" would not allow it to be told. As noted before, 1934–1936 represented one of the high points of a speculative business with fluctuating profits. Had Professor Herzog permitted the companies to present figures for the 1927–1936 period—the only fair standard—the books, fairly examined, would have shown an average net profit of 4.25 per cent a year; which was exactly the yield of United States government bonds during our period of prosperity. Basing the statement, presumably, on that "16.81 per cent profit," the Herzog report

declared flatly that the petroleum companies had long ago
paid off their capital investment—presumably while paying also a reasonable profit to the investors—whereas
every expert in the finances of oil knows that the American, British and Dutch pioneers sank countless millions
of dollars without profit in exploring the Mexican fields,
and that the petroleum business in the territory of our
interesting Southern neighbor has broken no better than
even.

The financial experts of the union arrived at these
figures—77,000,000 pesos in reserves and surplus, 16.81
per cent average net yearly profits for 1934–1936—by an
orgy of bad and biased accountancy. The most glaring
violation of all business rules, probably, lay in their
calculation of gross revenues. They had taken the total
production in barrels or gallons and multiplied it by the
current rates as quoted in the trade journals. Those were
not the actual prices at which the companies made their
sales but the "asked" prices. Any business man knows
the practical distinction. And from the difference between
these fanciful prices and the actual prices the report drew
the deduction that the companies were in a conspiracy to
undermanifest the value of their sales and thus conceal
revenues. So the report was able to add more than
43,000,000 pesos to the annual "profits" of the business.
In a manner just as arbitrary, it threw out many heavy
and legitimate expenditures, usually for "overhead,"
which good accounting practice recognizes as legitimate.
By elaborate though hazy reasoning, its authors justified
themselves in deducting from expenses the payments for
many of the complex taxes which the Mexican government had spread like a web about the petroleum business.
It juggled ingeniously the figures on intercompany trans-

actions. It even made mistakes in simple arithmetic—by strange coincidence always to the disadvantage of the companies—and in one case it confused a "credit" with a "charge."

Apparently, even this did not go far enough to meet the wishes of the Labor Board. When afterward they reviewed and revised Professor Herzog's report, they ruled, with an appearance of fairness, that one company had proved its protest against some of the charges of swollen profit made by the government's accountants, but added:

> Their reasons should not be given weight, in determining costs, to the degree set forth in their financial statements.

Another company had two subsidiary branches—one extracting petroleum, one refining and marketing it. The Labor Board, in jacking up Herzog's figures, alleged that the refining company had bought its crude oil from the producing company at a price lower than current market value; therefore, the Board added several million pesos to its hypothetical profits. But they refused flatly to deduct the corresponding sum from the receipts of the producing company which sold the oil!

On the basis of Herzog's original and unrevised figures, the experts' commission calculated casually that the "economic capacity" of the companies would permit them to pay increased wages and "social benefits" amounting to 26,000,000 extra pesos a year. It recommended this increase; it even went extensively into details, creating a revised wage scale for all classes of labor, whether overall or white-collar. Noticeably the greatest increases were in the lower ranks—in this, expressing the "leveling" tendency of communism and similar social creeds.

The figure of 26,000,000 pesos as the annual cost of this proposed rise in wages and increase in social benefits was another packful of jokers. The experts for the companies took up the items and calculated their real cost. They amounted to more than 40,000,000 pesos a year. And the total average net profit of the Mexican petroleum business was in this period only 23,000,000 pesos a year! The specter of confiscation was growing more substantial.

And all this time the government had two ways to prove exactly and fairly the actual profits and financial conditions of the companies. It could have appointed an *interventor* (receiver); and the inspection would have been up to the courts. It could have taken over the operation of the industry temporarily and found out for itself. It had chosen instead, the method of putting the matter to a Board whose personal bias would lead it to an inevitable conclusion.

The companies had seventy-two hours to answer this massive, complex and tricky document—an indictment and a sentence all at once. Perhaps the details of their brief do not much matter, now that the affair is so long past. They criticized and corrected false and juggled figures. They answered some of Professor Herzog's most palpable and dangerous misstatements. They wasted much good paper in protesting against the "management clauses" in the labor contract which Professor Herzog recommended. These were stiffer even than those contained in the original demands of the union. If granted, they would have made operation of the petroleum industry impossible—it would have fallen to chaos in a month. As the attorneys for the companies summed it up:

> The petroleum industry has on innumerable occasions made
> every effort to grant its workers conditions not equalled

today by any other industry in the republic. This policy
was consciously designed to procure harmonious relations
between employers and employees, and thereby effect a steady
development of the industry which would bring benefits to
the oil workers and their families, as well as to the com-
munities in which these activities are located, to the Federal,
state, and municipal governments, to the nation as a whole,
and, last but not least, to the shareholders who have made
the oil industry possible in Mexico . . . The petroleum
companies state in clear and precise language that they cannot
accept the responsibilities for this economic controversy . . .
for they believe in all sincerity that under the conditions out-
lined by the official commission their continuance in the country would be rendered economically impossible.

Following the procedure laid down in the labor laws,
the next stage would have been a hearing before the full
Labor Board, which would take up the report and consider testimony and arguments pro and con. But again
the Board evaded the task. Why, no outsider knows to
this day. Perhaps it shrank from the mighty labors involved. Perhaps it was trying to evade historic responsibility for an especially raw deal. And perhaps Cardenas
was in one of his hesitant moods. At any rate, it referred
the whole controversy to a kind of committee operating
under the Labor Board and known as "Group Seven."
This proceeding violated both the spirit and the letter of
the labor laws. Such boards may legally be formed to adjudicate the disputes of an industry operating in a single
state; but not those of an industry which is national in
the scope of its operations. But already the spirit of the
proceeding had run beyond such trifling considerations as
legal restraints. So three men constituting Group Seven
took over the job—one member representing labor, one
the companies and one the government.

On any fair three-man committee of arbitration, each party to the controversy has one representative while the third man is a neutral, unbiased outsider. In this case, every proceeding at every stage of the game, including especially that subtly-timed expropriation act—now hanging like a sword on a hair over the heads of the companies—had proved that the attitude and intention of the government and the unions were identical. It was as though a three-man commission to settle the Spanish Civil War had comprised one representative of the loyalists, one of the insurgents and either Stalin or Mussolini —take your choice. From a committee so composed, any observer might expect only a monotonous vote of two to one against the foreign petroleum companies. This one lived up to expectations. The companies protested, but the Labor Board ruled promptly and flatly that Group Seven was competent.

There followed two months of hearings, arguments, junkets to the properties of the companies, a rehash of all the facts and misrepresentations, truths and lies, charges and refutations, which had marked the hearings before the commission of experts. From the first, the handpicked majority of Group Seven showed its bias— although sometimes, when the proceeding seemed in retrospect a little too raw, it reversed itself. For example, the Group voted two to one generally to restrict the evidence which the companies might present and specifically forbade them to introduce their books and accounts. Later, it admitted the books—since the financial condition of the companies was the kernel of the question, this position had grown untenable. The companies asked that the union auditors and financial experts be called to the stand to explain how they arrived at their totals in the matter of surplus reserves and net profits. "Authorities cannot be questioned," ruled the chairman of the Board. This, of course, amounted to testimony without cross-examination, a defiance of law in any democratic land. But the majority ruled that the companies might submit to the opposing experts a written questionnaire.

It was the best they could do in the circumstances. Therefore, they prepared 143 most embarrassing questions and submitted them, as permitted. The reply came back with suspicious promptness. About fifty items were dismissed unanswered on the grounds that the experts' commission had gone out of existence on August 3rd, the day when it submitted its report, and these questions involved new issues. To many others, the union experts returned the comment "the answer is to be found in the report itself." Still others bore as answer a citation from the labor law: "A commission of experts shall formulate a report in the form which, as it appears to them, will effectively solve the conflict and prevent any repetition." The few questions answered specifically were inconsequential. Not a line to explain or to defend the antics of the actuaries in arriving at their false statements on reserves and profits! Finally, and most importantly, the demands of the striking unions and Professor Herzog's proposed settlement had both been drawn carelessly, especially in the passages relating to "social benefits." Several such benefits, required by Mexican law and granted accordingly by the companies, were not mentioned in either document. Did the unions and Herzog intend to waive these provisions of the law—asked the companies—or must they still be enforced? This meant a difference of a good many million pesos in the annual outlay. Opposite reasonable request for clarification on this point stood the monotonous reply "the answer will be found in the report itself." The answers to 143 questions, mostly technical, occupied ten typewritten pages. But Group Seven, by the conventional vote of two to one, found them quite satisfactory.

Again, after the commission of experts submitted its report of August 3rd, the companies and the unions, as stated before, had seventy-two hours to file any objections, which must be backed up by expert proof. The union had filed objections but submitted no proof. On August 12th, Group Seven ruled according to law that labor had lost its right to present expert evidence or to intervene in the proceedings; but when the Group settled down to business, experts for the unions appeared just the same, and the chairman—over the protests of the companies' representative of course—ruled that they might testify.

So Group Seven went over the same old ground and got really nowhere. On October 20, 1927, Lic. Gustavo Corona, chairman and government representative, snapped off the proceeding abruptly. Under the law, both sides had seventy-two hours to submit briefs. Both complied. It was now squarely up to the Labor Board—or to Group Seven. According to the Mexican Labor Law, the Board must:

> Dictate the award putting a definite end to the conflict, basing this decision upon the reports and findings of the experts' commission and upon the objections and proofs presented by the parties. The decision rendered on these terms shall have the same status and shall produce the same legal effects as an arbitral award.

Also, the law states flatly and specifically that the Board must hand down its decision within seventy-two hours after the litigants file their briefs.

The seventy-two hours passed—no decision. A week—no decision. Two weeks, a month, seven weeks, and still the Board and the two interlocked representatives on Group Seven kept mysterious silence. Why, no one outside of the inner circle of the Mexican government knows as yet. Perhaps no one but President Cardenas. The political labor leaders grew restless. Orators made fiery speeches before public meetings; there were demonstrations and threats. Finally, as Christmas of 1937 approached, the Petroleum Union called, by way of protest, a twenty-four-hour *paro* (illegal cessation of work) in certain key-locals. This affair showed signs of passing into the stage of organized disorder. President Cardenas telegraphed to the union leaders threatening the "penalty of the law"—which meant sending down the Army—if they did not keep the men at work. He must have dispatched private messages to other quarters; for the Labor Board announced abruptly that the decision would be handed down on December 18th.

The manner of imparting this decision was perhaps the oddest and most arbitrary feature in all these irregular proceedings. Señor Corona, as chairman, called Group Seven together, with secretaries and stenographers. The "proposed" decision was all ready. Neither the representative of capital nor that of labor had an inkling of the contents of the 1,000-page document which he laid out on the table. But there it was. The Group was to hear it read, to vote on it, section by section, without debate, and to finish the job that day. For more than ten hours the clerk read and the members voted—monotonously, two "ayes," one "no." It went through exactly as written. And when they had finished, the representative of the company must have felt like a lawyer who sits in court and witnesses his client being sentenced successively to 100 lashes, to the stocks, the electric chair, the gallows, the garrote and the guillotine.

The "verdict" in this star-chamber proceeding differed from the original demand of the union only in detail. Generally speaking, it endorsed the plan laid down by Professor Herzog when he drew up the experts' report. Some of the more absurd items were missing, it is true; and the demands for increase in wages were less fantastic. On the other hand, the terms regarding union participation in the management were far more severe; someone had subtly arranged them to give an appearance of fairness while making it impossible for a petroleum company to have much voice in the management of its own business.

It began by confirming Professor Herzog's ridiculously inaccurate statements as to the profits, reserves and surplus of the petroleum companies. It repeated his accusation that the companies had conspired to doctor their books in order to conceal "enormous profits." From this, it proceeded to the conventional harangue against these parasites who were "bleeding Mexico."

Getting down to the heart of the matter, it revised in detail the wage scale proposed by the commission of experts. But the sum total was almost the same—to be exact, a raise of 26,329,393 pesos a year. This, according to the calculation of the Board. The real cost still stood at more than 40,000,000 pesos a year.

With the exception of wage scales, it confirmed, in principle at least, virtually all of the important demands of the union as embraced in that bizarre ultimatum which opened this struggle—the forty-hour week with fifty-six-hour pay, the free medical care for hordes of relations, the excessive holidays, vacations and leaves of absence "on

demand" but on full pay, the unprecedented increase in
allowance for overtime, the financial support of union
offices, the right of the unions to veto reduction in personnel and to dictate building plans. But on its way through
the various boards, bureaus and groups, the contract had
taken on some extra frills and sustained some modifica-
tions—a few of them slightly in favor of the companies,
the rest decidedly in disfavor. The most important addi-
tions and alterations were as follows:

The companies must pay double for straight, ordinary
overtime, with a slight addition in case it was also night
work. For work on "weekly rest days," "obligatory rest
days" and holidays, triple pay; whenever any days in any
of these categories happened to coincide, quadruple pay.

For work at heights of ten meters or more above safety
platforms, at temperatures above 113 degrees f. within
installations, in places where there was an "excess of
gas in the air, or water, or oil on the ground," the companies must give double pay.

Any worker employed in the industry for less than
ten years must receive an annual vacation on full pay of
twenty-one working days; which amounted, adding in
week-ends and holidays, to about four weeks. After ten
years of service, they must receive thirty-one days on the
same terms. Wages for the vacation period must be paid
in advance.

The companies must grant sixteen holidays a year on
full pay—four of them national, twelve of them religious.

These terms, extreme as they must appear to any
open-minded reader, seem mild compared with the provisions for "increased social benefits." We must recall
again that the petroleum companies had for thirty years
given all employees and their immediate families free

medical care, including the services of specialists and good modern hospitals. To the original demands of the union —"grandmother clause" and all—this award added an order that they must erect additional hospitals wherever and whenever the National Mixed Commission—hereafter to be described—so ordered.

Beyond elaborate and expensive requirements for retirement and disability pay or pension, the award ordered special benefits for the victims of "occupational diseases." These it listed specifically. They included such illnesses as tuberculosis, pneumonia, pleurisy and malaria, no matter how, when or where acquired. Let us pause to consider malaria. It is endemic in the eastern coastal regions. The companies recognized from the first that they must make these jungles safe for man. Wherever they began drilling for a well or ran a pipe line, they drained away all standing water and cut all protective brush within flying range of the villainous she-mosquito which is the sole carrier of this disease. So far as their zone of operations was concerned, they had reduced the danger almost to nothing. They could not dictate as to the employee's movements during his hours of leisure. Under the terms of this award, a man going fishing on a holiday, or visiting a cousin on his vacation, might at a point far removed from company territory suffer the bite of a "bad" mosquito, acquire malaria, and receive the benefits of full pay during his illness and convalescence up to eighteen months. Tuberculosis may or may not be an occupational disease. But nowhere in the oil fields did the companies maintain living or working conditions tending toward development of the white plague. The same goes for pneumonia and pleurisy.

In case of disablement through accident or illness from a "non-vocational" cause, the employee must, after a three-day waiting period, receive eighty per cent of his regular pay—up to a maximum of 120 days in any twelve months' period.

In case of death from a non-occupational cause, the company must give the family of the deceased thirty days' pay. In case of death from an occupational cause, the death benefit became 1,280 days' pay. To a man totally disabled, the company must grant 1,460 days' full pay.

Each permanent employee must have his life insured for 4,000 pesos, his company paying half of the premiums.

Already the companies were maintaining savings funds for the benefit of their permanent employees. It was now ordered that the workers must pay ten per cent of their pay into these funds; and the companies must match them peso for peso. This, of course, raised still further the extraordinarily high wage scale which the companies must now pay.

To superannuated or disabled workers, the companies must pay life pensions of from sixty-five to eighty per cent of their wages on retirement. When such a pensioner died, the companies must pay his family thirty days' wages by way of funeral expenses.

In addition to day schools for the children of their workers, the companies must furnish night schools for adults. They must also educate a certain number of employees or their sons technically, either in Mexico or abroad.

They must furnish overalls and the laundering of the same for all workers. In cases of cold weather, rainy weather or excess oil on the surface of ground where men were working, they must furnish on demand all necessary clothing such as jackets, trousers and waterproof boots.

When a man took his three days' leave of absence on full pay for the purpose of doing some shopping in town, the company must pay for his transportation. The clause requiring the company to pay any employee's first-class transportation to any point, whenever he went on vacation, had stood up against a year of hammering. In spite of its absurdity, it remained in the final terms. And so on!

In the section on "management," however, this document concentrated most of its sting. In practical effect, the companies had three years to replace all their foreign technicians by Mexicans. It may be mentioned in passing that the old government-owned oil company found itself obliged to employ foreign chemists, petroleum engineers and the like, for lack of such in Mexico. Very well—let the companies train them—in three years! After a budding American chemist or petroleum engineer leaves preparatory school, he takes a four-year course in a university or technical institute, often spends two or three more years getting a higher degree, and does a few years of practical work before he qualifies as a real expert. Moreover his promotion to the higher executive positions goes by merit. In the proposed setup of the Mexican petroleum industry, merit, it seemed, had little to do with the case; for in the last analysis the union or the government would have the say as to selection and promotion of experts and would quite naturally choose on the basis of usefulness to the labor leaders or to the other politicians. The ultimatum of the unions had distinguished between "confidential" employees, responsible to the management for their acts, and unionized employees. This final arrangement permitted the chiefs of departments to rate in the "confidential" class, but only for the time being. Virtually all the assistants to chiefs of departments were "unionized" as were innumerable other smaller but vital employees. To take one example: The physician at the head of the medical department for any company might be a confidential employee, although he must be a Mexican citizen by birth. The rest of the doctors, nurses and hospital attendants must be union men or women and as such work under the "Exclusion Clause" which meant ostracism and perhaps starvation in case they disobeyed the orders of a union leader. And to make assurance doubly sure, it was provided that any executive against whom three members of a union made formal complaint, must be discharged. Analyzing this award of Group Seven at leisure, the representatives of the companies came to the conclusion that in three years or so the only foreigner left on the staff of any company would be its general manager, by which time every native Mexican employee would stand responsible not to the management but to the union or the government. To insure this result, the award provided that a mixed commission composed, like Group Seven itself, in such manner as to give the government and the unions a perpetual majority, should adjudicate all disputes between capital and labor. Final jab: The companies must pay their employees full wages for the time lost in the general petroleum strike of May, 1937.

The companies had only two arrows left in their quiver—weak missiles both. They could protest to the Mexican public and they could appeal to the Supreme Court. Their protest reviewed some of the injustices and absurdities already described. And it ended:

The oil companies have done everything in their power to bring about a fair and equitable settlement of this whole question. They sympathize with the known wishes of the President to raise the general standard of living and have already granted to their workmen wages and social benefits far in excess of those ruling in any other industry in the country, and have further offered substantially to improve this already high level.

In view of the foregoing, the oil companies formally state that they cannot accept the responsibility for the consequences which may arise from the present situation, and that they will be forced to take all necessary steps to safeguard their rights.

And they made a stand in the last ditch. On the ground of a dozen irregularities and plain violations of law which had marked the proceedings of the Labor Board and Group Seven, they applied to the Supreme Court for an *amparo* (injunction) to prevent the award from taking effect. Which makes pertinent a dissertation on the high court of Mexican justice.

In common with most Latin Americans, the well-educated Mexican tends to put his learning to theoretical rather than practical uses. Few English-speaking inhabitants of the Americas appreciate the wealth of scholarship in the countries south of the Rio Grande. The petroleum industry is a case in point. Mexico has enough good geologists to provide in that respect for any possible expansion of oil extraction, but she is short on the men who combine theoretical scholarship with practical experience—men who can plan and supervise such work as drilling wells or "cracking" petroleum. Following this rule, she has excellent lawyers; the standards of her bar are high. Until 1934, the Supreme Court was organized on a plan resembling our own—life tenure and choice for a reputation in the profession rather than for political considerations. In all the disturbed conditions between 1911 and 1934, it seemed like a rock of stability. At least three times during this period, it showed courage and independence by decisions which prevented Presidents from wholesale seizure of foreign property.

Cardenas had no sooner come to power than he showed himself determined to rid the Executive of this incumbrance. Just before his inauguration in 1934 the Constitution had been amended to give the President a six-year term. On assuming office, he rammed through another amendment, putting the Supreme Court at the mercy of the President. The term of service was limited to six years, running concurrently with the term of the President, who had the power of removing justices at will. He followed this by "cleaning out" the Court and appointing to the vacancy men sympathetic with his policies and his party.

The tribunal so constituted took under advisement the *amparo* of the oil companies. Mexican law has its peculiarities, of course. The Supreme Court does not decide such cases with a full bench, but delegates them to a Labor Court of five of its members. In this sub-Court sat the learned and violent Justice Xavier Icaza, another queer figure upheaved by the revolution. The only fact about Icaza pertinent to this story is his friendship and close association with Professor Lombardo Toledano, ultra-radical leader of Mexican labor, whose social views the Justice evidently shares. All through this long crisis Toledano had been raging against the companies with voice and pen; and Icaza had taken no pains to conceal his sympathies. The companies demanded that he, as a prejudiced party, disassociate himself from the proceedings—and for the moment got nowhere, as usual.

Meantime, the *amparo* had held up execution of the award. The Labor Board made this official on December 31, 1937. By now the pattern of confiscation had become so apparent that, in the spirit of a man who hides his wallet while the bandit is in the process of rifling the safe, the companies proceeded to get out of the country as much of their own ready cash as they could.

For the next two months, the Supreme Court sat on the case, scanning and considering thousands on thousands of pages of testimony, while the unions and the radical elements poured vitriol on the heads of the "foreign imperialists." Unofficially, the companies went into a series of negotiations with the Cardenas government. In the end, they made an offer which seemed almost self-ruinous. The Labor Board award had mulcted them for 26,000,000 pesos a year in increased wages and social benefits. Very well, they would assume that burden. But the increase must be limited to the stated sum—it will be remembered that the award of 26,000,000 pesos, when calculated in detail by honest accounting, meant really more than 40,000,000. That would amount to 3,000,000 pesos a year more than the current net profits of all the companies. By strict economies, by taking chances with their future, they might meet this increase in expenses and with luck break just about even. So they could at least keep intact their valuable properties, hoping that something would turn up. But the "management clauses" must be so amended as to give them some say in the operation of their own business. The Cardenas government turned this offer down, flatly and finally.

The Court opened its serious study of the documents in the case on February 2, 1938. Three days later, the radical forces began moving up their heavy guns. The

Communist-swayed Toledano drew up for the Union of Petroleum Workers a "program of agitation" designed to bully and browbeat the Justices. This the union adopted and put into operation—meetings, speeches, circulars, processions with banners and transparencies. An old transaction mentioned in a previous chapter came vividly into the news of the day. Repeating it: Nearly twenty years before, during the very depths of chaos in Mexico, a kind of bandit-general descended on the oil fields, took possession of the country, and demanded that the companies, on penalty of fire and sword, pay for the equipment of his forces. It was a plain holdup. The American companies stalled while they consulted the existing government in the City of Mexico and our own State Department. Both advised them to pay—it seemed the only way to save the wells. They did pay. The radical orators warped this transaction into a charge that the foreign companies had financed a revolution. They repeated the juggled figures of the experts' commission—sixteen per cent annual profit and the like—until the average Mexican worker who thought about the matter at all, probably believed them as gospel. Leaving the British and the Dutch companies out of the picture, they charged that these American companies, which had so long "looted Mexico," were only the entering wedge for invasion of the country by greedy Uncle Sam.

Exactly at this period, Mexico experienced a new spurt of hard times. The reasons were plain for all to see. The Cardenas policy of expropriating and dividing landed property wholesale was not working well. The ex-peon, given the right to work a farm, tended to raise upon it only enough produce to keep his family in food, and to let the rest lie fallow. With only a modicum of her available lands under cultivation, Mexico was importing still more Indian corn. Cardenas had nationalized the important sisal industry of Yucatan; and the production of sisal hemp had fallen almost fifty per cent. Mexican bonds of all classes had been so long in default that the government could borrow money neither at home nor abroad. It had exhausted its credit with the Bank of Mexico through heavy overdrafts to finance its social experiments. The radical orators and pamphleteers took advantage of this situation at once. They laid it all to the billions of pesos supposedly drained from the country by the "foreign pirates." When the Federation of Mexican Workers met in the capital on February 22, 1938, Toledano squarely charged the companies with sole responsibility for the "critical situation of the country." President Cardenas sprang a surprise by appearing before the convention to charge that the oil companies, when they withdrew their ready money from the banks, "restricted credit" and drove the country into the current depression. As a matter of cold fact, when in August 1937, the inquiry as to "economic capacity to pay" began before Professor Herzog and the expert's commission, Mexican capitalists smelt expropriation and began sending money out of the country. This movement swelled into a panic—a flight of capital to the amount of 85,000,000 pesos. The oil companies did not start sending away their own funds until December, when the Supreme Court upheld the decision of the Labor Board; and the sum involved was estimated at not more than five per cent of the total. A bizarre touch: Justice Icaza, sitting on the Labor Court of the Supreme Bench, which was adjudicating this case, played a leading part in the agitation. Translate that into American terms—the N.R.A., say, before the Supreme Court and Justice Stone or Justice Roberts writing letters denouncing the law to *The New York Times* or tearing the hide off from it before enthusiastic public meetings!

The farce played itself out on March 1st, when the Supreme Court met to hear the decision on the *amparo*. Labor leaders and delegations, carrying banners lettered with legends hostile to the companies, packed the Chamber. At this point, Justice Icaza did the unexpected. He arose and in a long, passionate speech, packed with charges against the companies, withdrew from the case. "I have already done my part," he said. "I have intervened continuously, firmly and passionately . . . It is not a conflict of a legal character but of a political character . . . I am satisfied with the manner in which I have behaved. I am even proud of it. . . . And once the small South American nations see what is happening in Mexico, they will do the same. . . ." After applause from the packed courtroom had died away, the Court listened to a "draft of decision" whose reading took four hours. It ruled against the companies on every point.

Usually, after the Mexican Supreme Court or one of its special panels hears such a "draft of decision," its members discuss the matter in hand publicly before proceeding to a vote. In this case, as soon as the reading was finished the presiding Justice announced that all the members were familiar with the draft and that there was no need for discussion. The Court thereupon proceeded to vote—four to nothing in favor of the "draft of decision" exactly as it stood. Justice Icaza's vote was not needed, as doubtless he knew when he withdrew from the case.

The Court passed sentence, briefly. The decision of the Labor Board was in no wise contrary to the Constitution.

The authorities might proceed to enforce the award. And that, again, was that.

The Board gave the companies a week—until March 7th—to acknowledge and to enforce the ruinous terms embraced in its new labor contract or automatically to declare themselves outlaws. They protested, of course— "The conditions recommended by the Official Commission which were made the basis of the award handed down by the Labor Board, are such as to make compliance impossible; the inability of the companies to comply has not been changed by the decision rendered today."

Searching Mexican law, the attorneys for the companies found a little loophole. To a District Court they applied for a "suspension of the effects of the award." The Court granted a temporary stay; but on March 12th it denied the application for a definite suspension. The companies appealed the decision to the Supreme Court. The papers in that process are still gathering dust among the archives. And again they notified the Labor Board that they could not possibly fulfill the terms of the contract. It was just at this juncture that, in the contemporaneous negotiations for settlement out of court, the government refused the tender of 26,000,000 pesos a year in increased wages and broke off all discussion.

Then the union appeared before the Labor Board with a charge that the petroleum companies were in *rebeldía*. Fix your mind on that bit of Spanish legal language. The word for "rebellion" in Spanish is *rebelion,* almost the same as ours. The word *rebeldía* is a bit of archaic language surviving only in the law—like "tort" in English. It signifies usually that one party to an action has failed to appear and has therefore forfeited his rights. Its rough equivalent in legal English is "default." But this similarity of two words seems to have given the astute Cardenas an opening for which he had been looking.

For this venture into domestic and international intrigue was not all such plain sailing as might seem from the foregoing account. From top to bottom, the business community of Mexico believed rightly that these elaborate maneuvers had for their object the expropriation of the oil companies; it saw only calamity ahead. The heavy tax on the petroleum industry stood as a financial mainstay for a government running every day further and further behind the game. The blight on the sisal industry and agricultural production in general showed what would probably happen as soon as the government took over. By now, the newspapers could offer little effective opposition; for in every office sat a censor authorized to "kill" anything tending to disturb the commonwealth or crimp government credit. But most of them exerted the power of passive resistance by blank silence on this controversy. The Army, always a power in Mexican politics, evidently did not like the prospect at all. However, the unions had their answer to that. Toledano had been organizing the unions into a kind of militia which drilled with arms on the plazas of the industrial towns.

When late in 1936 Congress passed the Expropriation Act authorizing the President to seize by decree the property of the petroleum companies, the Mexican Bar Association declared flatly, ". . . if the proposed law intends to authorize the expropriation of the elements of a mercantile or industrial business or of the business itself, clearly it is unconstitutional . . . the unconstitutionality of the project consists first in the private individual being despoiled of his property without trial by a duly constituted court and secondly, the executive power becomes the judicial power, thereby violating Articles 49 and 89 of the Constitution." And although the lawyers as a body were now keeping discreet silence, Cardenas must have known that the opinion of the majority among them had not changed in the least. Systematic agitation on the part of the unions and the radical element had served, however, as a counterfoil to prevent revolution—the constant apprehension of a Mexican President. In the perverted use of this word *"rebeldía"* Cardenas, who by now realized that he could no longer resist the urgent demands of the labor leaders for immediate, drastic action, saw apparently a bit of fuel to raise the temperature of his following from fever heat to white heat and so to frighten away any objectors to what he must do and now intended to do. Here also was a device to give an arbitrary transaction the counterfeit semblance of a moral justification. On March 18th, the Labor Board, as expected, declared that the companies were in *rebeldía*. A few hours later, Cardenas definitely cut the thread which held the sword suspended. In a decree breathing hate, he artistically slipped the real meaning of *rebeldía* into the false one of "rebellion" (after all, how many of his followers would know the difference?) and called the petroleum companies insurgents against the Mexican state. Wherefore, making effectual by decree the law of November, 1936, he declared that all properties of the petroleum companies were therewith and forthwith the property of the republic. That night, he defended his position in an eloquent speech over the radio.

Next morning the union, with the Army potentially behind it, moved on the oil properties. They grabbed everything—wells, pipe lines, refineries, buildings, docks, housing, residences, recreation halls and fields—everything except the fleets of tankers, which did not legally belong to the Mexican oil companies and which had withdrawn into extra-territorial waters as an added precaution. They rifled the safes. They opened the incoming mail and seized checks—even those which constituted payment for goods delivered as much as three months before. Both the actions-at-law and the decrees had for some reason omitted mention of several small foreign-owned companies. That made no difference; the unions, backed by the Federal power, seized most of these properties just the same. All foreign personnel was given forty-eight hours to leave the petroleum-bearing region. The foreigners had already closed their affairs and begun to pack. Out of the East Coast streamed a melancholy exodus —men and women to whom Mexico, for all her wrongs against them, was the beloved home. Some scattered to new fields; some, in the hope of seeing eventual justice done, joined the colony of the dispossessed in Mexico City.

*   *   *   *

This rapid summary of the illegally legal proceedings by which the Mexican government despoiled the oil companies has ignored, for the sake of clarity, certain minor actions-at-law. They are not essential to the main story and the result was always the same—a string of goose eggs for the petroleum companies. It may be worth while, however, to review this expropriation decree in the light of the Mexican Constitution.

Its governing provisions as regards public and private property declare that all subsoil resources such as mineral

veins and petroleum deposits are the property of the
nation. But it exempts specifically all such deposits to
which legal title was acquired before May 1, 1917. The
petroleum companies acquired virtually all their titles
before that date. Several times before Cardenas came
into power, decisions of the Supreme Court confirmed
that principle.

Article 16 orders flatly that no one shall be molested
in regard to his possessions except by written mandate
from competent authority in which the reasons for the
legal causes of the proceedings are cited.

The preamble of Article 27 forbids expropriation
without indemnification.

Article 28 prohibits the government from establishing
and operating an industrial monopoly.

Search the Constitution as narrowly as you will, you
will find no line, phrase or word contradicting these principles. The Expropriation Act is as clear a violation of
the Mexican Constitution as an act of our Congress sup-
pressing newspapers or forbidding the free practice of
religion would be of our own fundamental law. It takes
no lawyer to see that.

CHAPTER V

"Mexico Knows How to Honor Her Obligations"

DURING all these proceedings, the Ambassadors and Ministers of the nations whose citizens and subjects were in process of being despoiled had perforce sat on the sidelines as mere interested observers. The controversy was still a domestic matter; by the accepted rules of diplomacy, foreign governments could not protest until the Mexican courts pronounced final judgment or the Executive took action. The seizure of the oil companies let down the bars. Whatever might have been passing under the boards, the first effective protest from the United States came not in words but in action. Under our Silver Purchase Act, the Treasury was buying the Mexican output at a price which held up the world market. As silver goes, so goes Mexico. Our virtual subsidy of this industry south of the Rio Grande had enabled President Cardenas to impose an export tax for support of his government without the serious consequences which such a levy usually entails. Nine days after he took over the oil fields, Cardenas was forced to announce that our Treasury had suspended silver purchases from Mexico and intended henceforth to buy its supply at a lower rate in the open market—although a few weeks later these purchases were resumed from a private source. Promptly, the Mexican peso went into a decline.

Cardenas responded by a touch of drama. The United States, he declared, wanted to drain Mexico of her blood. Very well, she would bleed! And he announced a popular loan to pay for the oil properties. Workingmen would lend their slender savings, women would give their jewels, business men would cut into their capital, to free her from "foreign imperialism." He followed this with demonstrations imitated from our Liberty Loan drives in the World War. Unions and radical societies marched in processions, dropping the aforementioned savings and jewels into hoppers. This, the priming, blazed beautifully. But the main charge, being very wet, failed to explode. No affluent Mexican, however patriotic, wanted any part of a government loan. At the moment the Treasury was ignoring a bonded external debt of approximately 970,000,000 pesos. The bonds had paid no interest for twelve years, and were being offered for sale in New York at between one and two per cent of their par value. An internal agrarian debt of about 1,800,000,000 pesos was going the same way. Lending money to the government, in these circumstances, would amount to a levy on capital. The ballyhoo raised 98,000 pesos in the City of Mexico and less than $1,000,000 American in all; then the "loan for freedom" became merely a futile little episode in past history.

The British and the Dutch made prompt and blunt protest. Ignoring for the present the actions of the United States government, let us carry this part of the story to its end. The European governments both took the same stand. The seizure of the oil properties, they maintained, was illegal and arbitrary from every point of view. Mex-

ico could repair the wrong effectively in only one way—
restore the properties to their former and rightful owners.
Cardenas did not honor the Dutch with a reply; but he
swung into an exchange of notes with the more powerful
British. These grew constantly sterner on the part of His
Majesty's government, more acrimonious on that of the
Mexican. Then, having built the background with care
and art, in June, 1938, Cardenas made what seemed a
daring move. All this time, the two nations had been
sparring over the question of British property destroyed
or damaged in the revolutions. Mexico had previously
agreed "in principle" to pay up on the instalment plan.
A payment due on January 1st was still in default. On May
11th, Britain had dunned Mexico. In its note, the Foreign
Office included a few remarks on the state of Mexican
finances in general, and referred to the extraordinary
amount of defaulted Mexican bonds held by British
subjects. Cardenas was protesting that the rape of the oil
fields constituted not confiscation but expropriation. The
Mexican government, he said, fully intended to pay the
owners—some day. A British note in reply took occasion
to remark that a country which had signally failed in
meeting its minor obligations had no right to add such an
enormous item to its indebtedness.

This gave Cardenas an opening to grow—officially—
very, very angry. He sent the British a check for £18,000
as a payment on the revolutionary claims. With it went
a note which breathed defiance and made sarcastic refer-
ences to the defaults on the war-debts. At the same time,
he recalled his Minister at London and closed the Lega-
tion. The British could do nothing but reply in kind. So
diplomatic relations were broken—on the initiative of the
injuring party, not the injured.

It was splendid domestic politics. Mexico loves nothing more than courage; and its President had defied the Empire upon which the sun never sets! The populace did not know, of course, that Cardenas was insulting a caged lion. Britain had at the moment larger anxieties. The tension in Europe was rising toward that breathtaking climax, the Black Week of September, 1938. Britain could waste little energy on a complication in the Western hemisphere. But that was not the strongest bar of the cage. The Monroe Doctrine has been interpreted to mean that the United States looks with an unfriendly eye not only on any attempt of European powers to acquire territory in the Americas, but on the use by them of brute force in collecting a debt or avenging insult. So the typical Mexican politician varied his standard act of pulling Uncle Sam's whiskers with an interlude in which he twisted the lion's tail.

In contrast with the British Foreign Office our State Department worked to achieve its objective indirectly rather than directly. An examination of the position taken by the two governments, however, makes it clear that the United States must logically arrive at the same point as that adopted by the British government, which is that the seizures are illegal, and that the only just settlement is one which returns the properties to their owners.

The State Department began with a note to the Cardenas government a week after the Mexicans seized the petroleum properties. This note is practically unknown to the public. There is some question whether it was ever delivered. It was never published in full as were later notes on the land question. However, Secretary Hull on March 30, 1938, gave out the substance, though not the full text of this initial communication. Somewhat recondensed, his statement ran as follows:

> During the past few years the Mexican government in pursuance of its national policy has expropriated and is continuing to expropriate the properties of citizens of other countries in Mexico and of its own citizens. Among these have been many hundreds of farms and other properties of American citizens . . . This government has not undertaken and does not undertake to question the right of the government of Mexico in the exercise of its sovereign power to expropriate properties within its jurisdiction. This government has, however, on numerous occasions and in the most friendly manner pointed out to the government of Mexico that in accordance with every principle of international law, of comity between nations and of equity, the properties of its nationals so expropriated are required to be paid for by compensation representing fair, assured and effective value to the nationals from whom these properties were taken.
>
> The recent expropriation by the Mexican government of oil properties belonging to American citizens is therefore but one incident in a long series of incidents of this character and accordingly raises no new question. The subject now under consideration between the government of the United States and the government of Mexico is the matter of compensation for various properties of American citizens expropriated in the past few years. . . .

Faced squarely with a demand for payment, Cardenas replied with vague but exquisitely phrased courtesy: "You may be sure, Mr. Ambassador, that Mexico will know how to honor its obligations of today and its obligations of yesterday."

This seemed like a hazy promise to pay. It was not satisfactory, of course. When our State Department asked for a more definite pledge, sarcasm and irony began to cloud the courteous language of the Mexican President. Meantime, a curious little episode brought attention momentarily back to the oil issue. Mexico City "heard" that the United States had admitted the entire justice of the Mexican position—that we intended gracefully to let the oil fields go. Finally the newspaper *Ultimas Noticias* printed it as a fact, giving as authority a high official of the Mexican government. Whereupon Ambassador Daniels issued to the press on April 12th a general denial. He added:

> This publication was called formally to the attention of the Foreign Office by a member of the Embassy, who was told that no such statement had been made.

To which the well-informed correspondent of *The New York Times* added:

> Authoritative diplomatic quarters said . . . that the United States reserved rights under Mr. Hull's statement and that it could later demand the return of the oil companies if the terms of the Mexican indemnity payments were unsatisfactory.

Then the controversy over agricultural lands resumed the center of the stage—informal negotiations all through the summer and early autumn, varied by exchanges of notes, usually given out to the press. The tone of the replies from the Mexican President changed gradually from courteous to sarcastic to an attitude verging on insult. He was writing, usually, with one eye on the gallery. Several times in the course of the negotiations over both land and oil, Cardenas preceded the dispatch of a note by a public speech wherein he told a cheering audience what defiance he was about to hurl at John Bull or Uncle Sam. As for the substance of these notes, he attempted to justify all his expropriations on the grounds of "public necessity." Mexico was creating a new world. In the process of change, individuals here and there must suffer for the common good. He never quite repudiated the idea of payment, although he tried by inference to make our demand seem like extortion by the greedy rich from the deserving poor. But payment just at present, he said, was impossible on account of the "economic condition" of the country. It all boiled down to the insubstantial substance of his original note—"Mexico will know how to honor its obligations." In both public notes and private negotiations, American diplomats proposed that the matter be arbitrated, either by the machinery provided in Pan American treaties or by the Hague Court. The Cardenas administration indignantly spurned such a settlement as a violation of national sovereignty. Nothing apparently was said about the oil claims.

In July, the Mexican Foreign Office, through the Minister, Eduardo Hay, shifted to new ground. It began to put its own interpretation on international law. First:

> My government maintains . . . that no principle, universally accepted in theory or recognized in practice, is found in international law which makes obligatory the payment of immediate compensation or even deferred compensation, for expropriations of a general and impersonal character, such as those which Mexico has carried out in effecting the redistribution of land.

That phrase "or even deferred compensation" looked remarkably like total repudiation. But this document went on to a piece of even more daring and original juggling. It recalled the principle of "equality of treatment" generally recognized in international law, and drew therefrom this inference:

> When the Mexican government decided to suspend its agrarian debt in the year 1930, the measure affected equally Mexicans and foreigners. If Mexico had paid only the former, she would have without doubt violated a rule of equity; if she had paid only the latter, to the exclusion of the nationals, she would have committed a similar irregularity . . .

> The demand for an unequal treatment is implicitly understood in your government's note since [it demands] payment to its nationals independently of what Mexico might decide to do with respect to her own citizens, and as your government is aware that ours finds itself unable to pay indemnity immediately to all those affected by the Agrarian Reform, upon insisting on the payment to North American landowners it demands, in reality, a special, privileged treatment which no one is receiving in Mexico.

Secretary Hull waited a month to reply. The document in which he came back at Mexico is among the strongest and sternest of recent American state papers. Too long to quote in full, it demolished the first of those singular contentions by citing international law with chapter and verse:

> The doctrine of just compensation for property taken originated long in advance of international law . . . One nation after another decided that it was fair and reasonable, equitable and right, to accompany a taking of property by payment of just compensation . . . Today [this principle] is embodied in all the constitutions of most countries of the world and of every republic of the American continent, and has been carried forward as an international doctrine in the universally recognized law of nations . . . If the principle enunciated by Foreign Minister Hay were to be generally followed, what citizen of one republic making his living in any other of the twenty republics of the Western hemisphere could have any assurance . . . that he and his family would

not be evicted from their home and bereft of all means of livelihood? Under such conditions, what guarantees of security could be offered which would induce the nationals of one country to invest savings in another country or even to do business with the nationals of another country?

The second and more original contention Mr. Hull polished off in a long passage from which we quote a few significant sentences:

> The doctrine of equality of treatment . . . is of ancient origin . . . The word has invariably referred to equality in lawful rights of the person and to protection in exercising such rights. There is now announced by your government the astonishing theory that this treasured and cherished principle of equality, designed to protect both human rights and property rights, is to be invoked, not in the protection of personal rights and liberties, but as a chief ground of depriving and stripping individuals of their conceded rights. It is contended, in a word, that it is wholly justifiable to deprive an individual of his rights if all other persons are equally deprived and if no victim is allowed to escape . . . The proposition scarcely requires answer.

Mr. Hull might have reduced this principle to further absurdity by imagining some violent and tyrannical government breaking loose and massacring a thousand of its subjects together with a hundred American citizens temporarily resident in the country. Under the doctrine of "equality of rights" as interpreted by Mexico, we could have no complaint, since the offending government had treated native and foreigner exactly alike.

This note of Secretary Hull, which will reassume importance when our State Department takes up the matter of the petroleum claims, ended open diplomacy in the matter of the expropriated lands. But secret negotiation went on. And in the late autumn of 1938, the governments reached an understanding. We had agreed openly to continue our silver purchases from Mexico with the old arrangement. Mexico now agreed to pay for the expropriated lands on the instalment plan—"if and when her financial condition permitted"—and at the rate of a million dollars, American, a year. And she promised to lay down on the counter the first instalment in June, 1939. As a business proposition, Mexico got more out of the agreement than the United States, since the export tax imposed on silver amounts to many times a million dollars a year. Mexico did not agree to stop expropriations, so in spite of the fact that the State Department almost abandoned its original position, the controversy over agricultural lands is settled temporarily. At least we have preserved one principle as a basis for negotiating the much more important controversy over the stolen oil wells—no appropriation without indemnification.

Unofficially, our State Department and the Mexican Foreign Office were all this time discussing the question of the expropriated oil fields. In the course of these negotiations, Mexico made one definite proposal. As will be shown hereafter, having lost the important and convenient American market for petroleum she was searching madly for new customers. Now, she proposed to pay off the debt in instalments by delivering each year to the foreign companies a certain definite amount of crude oil—extracted, of course, from their own properties. This proposal was unsound both morally and practically. Morally, it implied paying for stolen goods with the usufruct thereof. Practically the supplies of crude oil lying underground were only a part of the property that Mexico had seized. Above ground, she had taken wharves, refineries, pipe lines, office buildings, whole villages of workmen's houses. Giving the companies all the oil underlying their properties, minus the amount necessary to pay the costs of extraction and transportation, might possibly have paid the debt—in the course of twenty, thirty or forty years. But the owners could have no assurance that Mexico would bring in wells from the lands covering known but undeveloped deposits and that she would not ruin such deposits by inexpert drilling and extraction—the record of the old Mexican-owned oil company was very bad in this respect. Further, they could not foresee the course of the markets. Under this impossible arrangement, Mexico might dump on to them millions of barrels of oil at a time when the market was glutted and prices ruinously low. Acceptance would have constituted an invitation to despoil American owners of property in all ruthless foreign countries. Further, experience had shown the difficulty of collecting a long-term obligation of this kind from any Mexican government of the past twenty years. The companies turned a cold shoulder to this proposal. In February, 1939, the date of writing, the matter had advanced no further than that. The United States still demanded payment and the Mexicans promised to pay—some time. Mexico has, in diplomatic language, "confessed inability to meet a legal expropriation." Translating the affair into terms of ordinary commercial intercourse, "why did you buy that diamond ring when you knew you couldn't pay for it?"—"Because I wanted it so much!" Considering that these oil properties are worth hundreds of millions of dollars, the confessed inability seems a real inability; in that, at least, the Mexican position approaches candor.

Although the State Department in its first note after the oil seizures linked oil expropriations with agricultural expropriations, there are certain fundamental differences between the two issues.

The sum involved in the expropriation of American-owned agricultural lands is so relatively small that almost any government capable of functioning could pay it. Furthermore, the tracts are scattered all over the republic. Victims of successive seizures over a long succession of years, the properties have often changed their character. Many of them have been broken up, and parcelled out among countless families. In other cases the inheritors have replaced old crops with new, or let the land go wild. It is probable that most of the original owners would not go back to their old ranches even if they had the opportunity.

The oil properties, on the other hand, form a vast, integrated unit which can still be returned relatively intact. If the action comes promptly, that is; otherwise awkward, political management may work irreparable damage to producing fields and to equipment. More and more, the logic of the situation is driving on toward the position which the British have held from the first, that the only fair and practical settlement is the return of the properties to their rightful owners.

To clear the air, it may be well to consider what is here meant by the word "owners." They are nominally and actually corporations; the Mexican agitator has made much of that fact. But who owns these corporations? Hundreds of thousands of stockholders, the vast majority in modest circumstances—the small professional man or cross-roads storekeeper of Indiana or Devonshire or Friesland, the thrifty stenographer of Chicago or London or Rotterdam, the mechanic saving up to educate his boys, the widow who has invested her husband's life in-

surance. These, not a set of legal entities called corporations, are the ultimate victims of this robbery masked by
the forms of law.

From the time when the Mexican government took over
the oil fields, it drew a curtain about them. None enters
that region unless he carries a pass; and the government
denies passes to all foreigners except those committed in
some form or other to the Cardenas plan of government.
It is certain, however, that production has declined ma-
terially—perhaps by as much as one-third. A foreigner
who slipped in and out of Tampico late in 1938, found the
town already down at the heel. Before March, when the
expropriation decree went into effect, twenty tankers a
week loaded and sailed from the port. Now it was lucky
to dispatch six or seven. Business was marking time.
Many shops and cafés had put up the shutters and unem-
ployed men lolled on the wharves.

Cardenas, when he seized the oil fields, doubtless expected to add the profits of the companies to the high
taxes they were paying, to sell off accumulated stock of
petroleum and petroleum products—at bargain rates if
necessary—and so to help himself through a financial
crisis. It is probable that this program has failed. The
Americans, British and Dutch of course withdrew at once
their fleets of oil tankers. The Mexicans had to scramble
for sea transport; almost certainly at excessive rates.
The expropriation cut off the American and British market. The Mexican government knew that all this would
happen; but there were Japan engaged in a war, and Germany creating an intensive armament. They would make,
theoretically, a splendid, eager market. However, there
is no oil production on the West Coast. After buying four
cargoes the Japanese calculated the extra mileage and

tolls involved in a haul through the Panama Canal, compared it with the cost of transportation from Oriental and Near Eastern fields, and lost interest.

Germany seemed the great potential market. The Nazi government would pay a little cash; the rest must be payment in kind—German goods for the Mexican government to sell in its own domestic market. If Germany lost by this bargain, it was the first time! When the blow fell and ex-chauffeurs, shift-bosses or unskilled politicians stepped into executive positions, experienced oil men prophesied that this nationalized business could not long keep up production without foreign experts. Already in exploring for new wells, it has had to employ many drilling-crews from Texas. When it finds itself tragically lacking in men capable of directing the larger operations of extraction or refining it cannot, of course, get Americans, Britons or Dutchmen—even if it wants to. Rumor in Mexico City has it that specialists sent by the Nazi government are at work in the oil fields. This may not be true at present; it may very well be true in the end. Where else can Mexico find exports? This commercial alliance between a government whose policies verge on communism and that totalitarian nation which makes capital of its opposition to both communism and democracy, is not the smallest anomaly in this odd situation.

The new management has not been able to command the chemicals necessary for production of modern, high-compression gasoline. Therefore the domestic supply is so unsatisfactory that the taxicab drivers are cursing it on the streets of Mexico City. The product of the refineries must be doctored abroad before it goes on to the foreign market; and so it must logically command a lower price than the four-square gasoline which the foreign companies used to ship abroad. The goose that laid the golden eggs may not be quite dead; but at best it is in very bad health.

As for the workers' paradise promised the employees of the petroleum industry, that, too, has probably proved to be a mirage. The new management has not maintained the efficient social services, such as medical care, sanitation and schools, which the foreign companies gave their employees. Hospitals and dispensaries, recreation halls, playgrounds and sanitation are already running down. Had the government raised wages to the scale which the unions demanded, Mexican propaganda would doubtless have trumpeted the news to the world. But on that point we have only one brief, chary and vague statement. An official talking to a foreign reporter made a remark which may be interpreted as meaning that after the expropriation the wage scale rose by nearly 5,000,000 pesos a year. This does not tell the whole story. Since the seizure of the oil fields the cost of living has risen thirty or forty per cent. The workmen are not drawing overtime pay. They have lost the privilege of free house rent. They are paying for social benefits which the companies used to give them free. As against that the reader may remember that the companies, in the final emergency, offered an increase in wages and social benefits of 26,000,000 pesos.

And another glimpse through the veil shows whom these increased wages—if any—are benefiting. An American once high in the management of the Tampico fields learned quite by accident that a certain important piece of executive work, which employed in his time two or at most three technicians, now enjoyed the paid services of about thirty men—mostly ex-politicians, ex-chauffeurs, ex-labor leaders, all but one or two without any previous training or experience in a highly technical process. None of them received a salary quite so large as that of the American experts whom they replaced, but the aggregate cost of their services was much greater. So far, probably, the politicians form the only class or interest in Mexico which has profited by the expropriation of the oil fields. It cannot have helped the commonwealth; it certainly has not helped the average worker at the wells, docks or factories.

At the end of 1938, the episode of oil expropriation in Mexico ceased to be a controversy limited to four interested nations. Mexico contrived to make it an international issue involving the whole Western hemisphere when at the Pan American Congress her delegates attempted to get the "Calvo Doctrine" endorsed and sanctioned. That principle has been mentioned before. Carlos Calvo was a distinguished Argentinian diplomat of the middle Nineteenth Century and a high authority on international law. He is now remembered mainly as author of a radical doctrine which held that an individual acquiring property in any country except his own should be regarded, in all matters relating to such holdings, as a citizen of the country where they lay. As a corollary, if he felt himself mistreated in matters affecting property so situated, the alien might not appeal to his own government for help and protection. Calvo did brilliant and original work in building up the recognized codes of international law. But his confrères of his own time and the overwhelming majority of critics in a later period regarded this as one of those fantastic hobbies which sometimes mar the sound work of an otherwise able man. Anti-foreign agitators in Latin America, however, kept the doctrine feebly alive until 1917, when Mexico "swallowing all formulas" in her new Constitution adopted the Calvo Doctrine lock, stock and barrel. If this law were universal, an American, Briton or a Mexican in a foreign land might be forced to hand over his property literally with a gun pointed at his head; and he would have no recourse save in courts, which might be controlled by the offending government. In 1925, the Mexican Congress passed an alien land law designed to put this article of the Constitution into effect, and the government forced virtually all foreign landholders, including the oil companies, to sign specific waivers of their rights as nationals.

But the United States government refused as it always has, to grant its nationals the power to sign away something which it contends belongs not to the citizen but to his government. From the moment when we had our first brush with the cantankerous Señor Carranza, the United States government declined to acknowledge the validity of the Calvo clause, and maintained this attitude through all of the negotiations with Obregón and Calles, until it finally became a dead-letter between the two countries. However, during the summer of 1938, Cardenas pulled the Calvo Doctrine out of the moth balls and wove it into his notes to the British Foreign Office. The British followed precedent by refusing to recognize it as valid.

It bobbed up again, however, when one of the Mexican delegates to the Pan American Congress—he has Communist leanings—offered a three-point program to "protect the Americas from imperialism," and resolutions designed to put it into force. The first point expressed the Calvo Doctrine in full. The second, a kind of corollary, required the nations of both Americas to recognize as valid any renunciation their own citizens might make regarding protection by their own governments; further it pledged the nations themselves not to offer protection in case of disputes over property between their nations and other American governments. The third clause looked comparatively innocent and commendable on the surface; but dynamite lay underneath. Mexico asked the Congress to adopt a "continental solidarity pact" providing in essence "that if the peace of any American state is menaced from without or within the continent by the direct or indirect interference of another state or by unofficial acts or activities which have support from another state, although they may not have the appearance of force, and which may change or subvert the national or political institutions of the threatened state, consultation shall always be initiated exclusively by the government of the threatened state." Coming from Mexico that mouthful of diplomatic language referred of course to the United States. It was a defiance, a hint of "financial imperialism," an invitation to loot the foreigner, all rolled into the same package.

And its implications, just now, are especially dangerous. The democracies—Great Britain, the United States and France—are in the aggregate the greatest foreign holders of investments in Latin America. The totalitarian governments are trying to break in with bilateral barter penetration in opposition to the principles of Secretary Hull's multilateral trade agreements.

If there should be a general confiscation of all property belonging to citizens of the democracies, the totalitarian governments might naturally be expected to seek to extend their influence. When and if that begins to happen in any other Latin American nation, Uncle Sam will have to hold the bag as he is holding it in Mexico, since the Monroe Doctrine has not only its manifest advantages but its heavy responsibilities. In face of it, no looted European

democracy could make any very effective protest and in
some fashion or other the victim would hold us responsible for action. But if this last principle of the three-point
program became a recognized principle of all statecraft
on the American continent, the offender could "initiate
consultation"—which might mean a combination of all
Latin America against any policy we might adopt.

The Pan American Conference in general did not regard these Mexican proposals very seriously. The Calvo
Doctrine and its corollary received virtually no support,
although a few radicals in one or two South American
delegations did come out in favor of proposition number
three. The Conference as a whole disposed of this troublesome matter by referring the Mexican program back to
committee. Better for the peace of the Americas if they
had brought it to the floor, debated it and let it go to its
certain defeat. Now it cannot come up again until 1943.
And in the meantime—well, the actions of the Mexican
delegation showed what we may expect. As soon as their
proposal went back to committee, they left Lima prema-
turely and joined a set of Mexican agents who traveled
fanwise to all the South American countries, with special
attention to those that produce oil. No one doubts what
goods they were selling. They were trying to get backing
for this three-point program. Further, they were advising
and encouraging the other nations to go and do likewise,
holding out the glittering temptation of something for
nothing. So, when we get ready to demand reparation for
the seizure of the oil fields they hope to present against us
a solid front—every nation south of the Rio Grande.

It is no longer merely a question of returning some hundreds of millions of dollars to men and women, American, British and Dutch, who have invested their savings

in an honest and useful commercial proposition. Now, the controversy involves our whole investment, amounting at lowest estimate to three and a half billion dollars in the Latin American countries, and the larger British investment for which the Monroe Doctrine makes us partially responsible. The merely commercial issue is even wider than that. Those totalitarian nations which constitute at this moment the real danger to the smaller and weaker countries of the Americas are everywhere sawing away at the foundations of our export trade. In Mexico they are buying oil which is really ours and paying for it not in cash but with "earmarked currency" good only in payment for commodities. So they are driving American manufactured goods, such as machinery, out of the Mexican market, and the movement is gradually spreading to embrace nearly all of Latin America.

Thus Mexico is extending the injuries inflicted on American citizens through direct confiscation of property by becoming the spear-head of a general attack on the legitimate interests of the United States throughout the Western hemisphere. Everything depends on the settlement of this controversy over the confiscation of the oil fields. From the Rio Grande to the Horn, shrewd eyes are watching us. If, good-naturedly and over-tolerantly, we let our claims on Mexico lapse, if, as so often in the past, we exchange substance for the unsubstantial shadows of insincere promises—their radical politicians, jingo-mongers, embarrassed governments in need of easy money and Nazi-Fascist or Communist intriguers will take heart of grace and move to action. The future of our foreign policy, perhaps the future of democracy in the Western hemisphere, depends on the strength or weakness, the wisdom or stupidity, of our actions in the present crisis.

APPENDIX A

Mexican Rulers Since Porfirio Diaz

May 26, 1911	Francisco Leon de la Barra (Provisional President)	Resigned.
Nov. 1, 1911	Francisco I. Madero	Assassinated.
Feb. 19, 1913	Pedro Lascurain (Provisional President for 28 minutes)	Resigned.
Feb. 19, 1913	Victoriano de la Huerta (Provisional President)	Exiled.
July 15, 1914	Francisco Carbajal (Provisional President)	Resigned.
Aug. 20, 1914	Venustiano Carranza (First Chief)	Deposed.
Nov. 10, 1914	Eulalio M. Gutierrez (Provisional President)	Exiled.
Jan. 16, 1915	Roque Gonzalez (Provisional President)	Exiled.
July 31, 1915	Francisco L. Chazarro (Provisional President)	Exiled.
Oct. 15, 1915	Venustiano Carranza (Provisional President)	Deposed.
Nov. 11, 1917	Venustiano Carranza	Assassinated.
May 25, 1920	Adolfo de la Huerta (Provisional President)	Exiled.
Dec. 1, 1920	Alvaro Obregón	Assassinated.
Dec. 1, 1924	Plutarco Calles	Exiled.
Dec. 1, 1928	Emilio Portes Gil (Provisional President)	Term expired.

Feb. 5, 1930	Pascual Ortiz Rubio	Assassination attempted.
Sept. 9, 1932	Abelardo Rodriguez	Term expired.
Dec. 1, 1934– To date	Lazaro Cardenas	

APPENDIX B

Insurrections in Mexico Since 1910

1910–1911— Madero Revolution. Resignation of Diaz. Francisco I. Madero assumes Presidency.

1913–Feb.— Revolution against Madero by Generals Felix Diaz and Bernardo Reyes. General Victoriano de la Huerta assumes Presidency.

1913–Mar.— Revolution against Huerta by Carranza.

1914–Aug.— Constitutionalist troops under Obregón enter Mexico City, followed by Carranza, who assumed title of "First Chief."

1914–Sept.— Villa revolt against Carranza.

1915–Mar.— Zapata enters Capital with his forces, after Carranza withdraws.

1915–Apr.— Carranza forces under Obregón defeat Villa at Celaya.

1915–July— Carranza troops under General Pablo Gonzalez recapture Mexico City.

1916–Mar.— Villa attacks town of Columbus, N. M., and U. S. Cavalry camps, killing seventeen. Pershing expedition enters Mexico.

1920–Apr.— Revolution against Carranza by de la Huerta and Obregón.

1929–Feb.–May— Escobar revolution against Portes Gil suppressed by General Calles.

APPENDIX C

Chronology of the Controversy Over Mexican Oil

1900—Exploration for oil begun by Americans and British.

1910—"Golden Lane," famous prolific oil field, discovered.

May 1, 1917—Mexican government nationalizes subsoil resources.

July 8, 1918 to Aug. 8, 1918 } Carranza Decrees define conditions under which exploration for and exploitation of natural resources might be effected.

1921—Mexico's production of oil reaches all-time peak.

1923—"Petromex," government-sponsored oil company, replaces National Administration of Petroleum Control.

1923—Agreement reached at "Bucareli Conference" between representatives of Mexico and United States that Mexico will pay just value in cash at time of taking for expropriated properties.

1924—Fear of increasing difficulties in Mexico diverts investment of new capital to other countries, notably Venezuela where intensification of oil development begins.

Dec. 26, 1925—Mexico's national petroleum law enacted.

1925—National Administration of Petroleum Control created as government oil agency.

1926—Commercial production of oil begins in Colombia.

Aug. 18, 1931—Federal labor law enacted.

1932—Mexican oil production shows continued decline at end of six-year period.

Dec. 1, 1934—Lazaro Cardenas becomes President of Mexico; announces six-year program of "nationalization" and economic reform.

Sept. 16, 1935—Government fixes domestic price of gasoline.

Feb. 11, 1936—President Cardenas, speaking at Monterrey during labor dispute, declares "industrialists who are weary of the social struggle can turn their industries over to the workmen or to the government."

Aug. 18, 1936—Law enacted requiring business firms to affiliate with Chambers of Commerce or Industry operating under government supervision.

Sept. 1, 1936—President Cardenas advances theory that industrial compliance with labor syndicates' demands should be limited only by "economic capacity."

Oct. 6, 1936—Mexican Bar Association attacks proposed expropriation bill.

Oct. 30, 1936—Luis Cabrera, leading Mexican publicist, denounces expropriation bill as a menace; says Mexico lacks capital of its own.

Nov. 3, 1936—Petroleum syndicate submits standard collective contract calling for increased wages, curtailed working hours, extensive additional social benefits, and company contributions to syndicate operating costs; calls strike for November 13th unless contracts accepted.

Nov. 13, 1936—Threatened general strike postponed six months at request of President Cardenas, who advises Syndicate to submit case to Federal Labor Board.

Nov. 23, 1936—Expropriation law confirmed.

Jan. 30, 1937—"National Petroleum Administration" established by Mexican Government to replace "Petromex."

May 8, 1937—Newspapers report visit of Mexico's Attorney

General to Supreme Court's chambers to urge "co-operation with government."

May 28, 1937—General strike in petroleum industry begins.

May 30, 1937—Federal Labor Board declares strike legal; holds oil companies responsible for "strike pay."

June 9, 1937—Syndicate refuses companies' compromise offer; fails to gain government support; strike lifted.

June 10, 1937—Syndicate petitions Federal Labor Board to investigate oil companies' "economic capacity."

June 11, 1937—Companies protest illegality of proceeding on jurisdictional grounds.

June 12, 1937—Federal Labor Board rejects companies' protest; appoints special committee (Group Seven) to handle case; names commission to investigate oil companies.

June 14, 1937—Presidential decree establishes governmental regulation of production, distribution, and sale of commodities.

Oct. 23, 1937—Investigating commission reports findings and recommendations to special group of Federal Labor Board.

Dec. 18, 1937—Special group of Federal Labor Board decides against companies and fixes award to Syndicate.

Dec. 28, 1937—Oil companies appeal to Mexican Supreme Court to set aside the award as making operations impossible, suggest compromise, protest to Federal Labor Board against handling of case by special group, and ask suspension of award.

Jan. 1, 1938—Companies file memorandum with U. S. Department of State explaining their position.

Jan. 6, 1938—Federal Labor Board refuses to suspend award.

Jan. 7, 1938—Companies appeal to Supreme Court against Federal Labor Board's denial of suspension.

Feb. 3, 1938—Syndicate leaders banquet Supreme Court Justice Icaza, judge of labor section.

Feb. 1938—Minister of Labor tenders official support to syndicalism.

Feb. 22, 1938—Lombardo Toledano, addressing Syndicate Confederation as secretary and attorney, predicts Supreme Court will rule against companies.

Feb. 24, 1938—President Cardenas tells Confederation foreign oil companies are trying to cause economic crisis.

Mar. 1, 1938—Companies challenge right of Justice Icaza to sit in case because of his prominent activities as Syndicate advisor. Justice Icaza asks to be excused from participation in case, and denounces oil companies. Mexican Supreme Court upholds Labor Board's decision.

Mar. 7, 1938—Companies obtain temporary stay suspending Federal Labor Board's decision for five days.

Mar. 12, 1938—Judge Bartlett of First District Court terminates stay, holding welfare of nation demands Federal Labor Board award be effectuated. Companies confer with President Cardenas; offer to pay portion of award if Syndicate demands regarding administrative positions are modified; compromises rejected.

Mar. 17, 1938—Syndicate petitions Labor Board to void all contracts with companies.

Mar. 18, 1938—11 A.M., Labor Board grants companies an injunction against Syndicate's action.

2:00 P.M., Labor Board reverses action, removes injunction, declares all contracts cancelled.

Evening, President Cardenas signs Executive Decree expropriating oil companies' properties.

Mar. 19, 1938—Company operations suspended.

Mar. 20, 1938—American personnel forced to evacuate offices and homes; gasoline shortage suspends travel.

Mar. 21, 1938—Government Administrative Council of Oil begins operation of expropriated properties.

British government informs Mexico that Britain reserves all its rights in the matter of expropriations.

Mar. 27, 1938—Silver purchase agreement between United States and Mexico suspended by Secretary Morgenthau.

Mar. 28–29, 1938—U. S. Treasury reduces price paid for foreign silver one cent each day.

Mar. 29, 1938—President Cardenas calls special session of Congress to authorize $20,000,000 internal loan to indemnify companies whose property seized; requests Congress modify export and import duties raised in January and protested by United States. Mexican government begins proceedings to attach company bank accounts.

Mar. 29, 1938—U. S. Secretary of State Hull announces United States insists upon payment of "fair assured, and effective value to the nationals" of seized properties.

Mar. 31, 1938—President Cardenas in a note couched in diplomatic terms of friendship tells Secretary of State Hull that Mexico "will know how to honor its obligations."

Apr. 5, 1938—Oil companies appeal to District Court at Mexico City for injunction, holding expropriation action violated Constitution.

Apr. 6, 1938—District Court at Mexico City fixes September 29, 1938, as date for hearing companies' appeals.

Apr. 8, 1938—Great Britain informs Mexican government expropriation is "inherently unjustified" and requests properties be restored.

Apr. 13, 1938—District Judge Ignacio Martinez denies companies' petition for injunction to set aside Labor Board decision suspending syndicate's contracts. Orders the companies to pay workers three months' "severance pay." President Cardenas instructs Minister of Finance Eduardo Suarez to proceed with appraisals of the expropriated properties.

Publication of Mexico's reply to British note suggests existence of "national emergency" through termination of labor contracts and upholds rights of expropriation on grounds of public interest.

Apr. 20, 1938—District Court at Mexico City moves forward to May 11th the September 29th date previously fixed for hearing companies' appeals against expropriation law and expropriation decree.

Apr. 21, 1938—British government reiterates that seizures are contrary to rules of normal international practice and repeats requests for return of oil properties.

May 10, 1938—British government requests immediate payment of its portion of claims for damages suffered by British nationals in Mexican revolutions.

May 11, 1938—Mexican District Court Judge Bartlett receives companies' appeals against expropriation law and expropriation decree. Takes appeals under advisement.

May 13, 1938—Mexico pays installment on British share of claims. Mexico withdraws its diplomatic representative from London in protest against "unfriendly attitude" of Great Britain.

May 14, 1938—British Minister to Mexico announces his early departure from Mexico in accordance with instructions from London.

June–Aug. 1938—Informal exchange of notes and views on land expropriations between the United States and Mexico.

July 21, 1938—Eduardo Hay, Mexican Foreign Minister, in note to Washington cites principle of "equality of treatment" as reason for deferring or cancelling payment of American land claims.

Aug. 22, 1938—Secretary of State Hull replying, calls contention of Hay an "astonishing principle" and demands full payment.

Nov. 12, 1938—Announcement that United States and Mexico have reached an agreement as to land claims.

United States Treasury resumes silver purchases.

Dec. 9–27, 1938—Pan American Congress at Lima. Mexican delegates present a program based on the "Calvo Doctrine" and designed to prevent alien property-owners in any country from appealing to their own governments in case of unjust treatment as regards their property. Mexican program referred back to committee.

Jan. 28, 1939—Mexican government reports that oil production for 1938 was 38,505,284 barrels compared to 46,906,560 in 1937, and oil exports 14,800,000 barrels in 1938 compared to 23,-972,483 in 1937.

INDEX

Anti-Americanism, 2, 14, 43, 47, 52, 93, 116, 125, 141

Bucareli Conference, 17, 56, 60

Calles, Elias Plutarco, 14, 16, 18–20, 54, 56, 59–60, 66–68, 140

Calvo Doctrine, 13, 139–140, 142

Cardenas' Promises to Pay, 1, 71, 128, 130, 133–134

Carranza, Venustiano, 12–14, 17, 47, 51–54, 63–65, 140

Commission of Experts, 94–95, 98–100, 104–105, 107, 117, 119
  Labor Union Experts, 99, 103–104
  Oil Company Experts, 94–95, 101
  Questionnaire to Companies, 95, 97
  Report to Labor Board, 97–101, 107

Communist Activities, 18–19, 63, 66, 94, 116, 140, 143

Confiscation, Trend toward, 13, 15, 17–22, 54–55, 67, 71, 80, 83, 92, 117, 120, 122, 126

Confirmatory Concessions, 56

Constitutions of Mexico, 13, 17, 19–20, 31–32, 34–35, 51–52, 55–56, 58, 64, 82, 91, 114, 118, 121–123, 139–140
  Non-Retroactive Clause, 18, 31, 35, 52–53, 55

Constitutional Convention, 64–65

Continental Solidarity Pact, 141

Corona, Gustavo, 105–106

Daniels, Josephus, 129

de la Huerta, Adolfo, 12, 14, 43, 54

Diaz, Porfirio, 7–9, 11–12, 15–16, 26, 29–30, 39, 50–51, 62–63, 90

"Economic Capacity" to Pay, 71, 79, 98, 100, 117

Economic Issue, 87, 92–93

Expropriation Act, 83, 120–121, 123
  Effect on Other Countries, 139, 143

Effect on U.S. Total Investments, 143

Fascist Influences, 19, 137, 143

Federal Department of Labor, 66, 83, 85

Federal Labor Board, 21, 70, 74, 82, 85, 87, 89, 92–94, 100–107, 113, 115, 117–119, 121
  Group Seven, 102–103, 105–106, 112–113
  Group Seven's Decision, 106–112

Federal Labor Law, 86–87, 105

Government-owned Oil Company, 7, 17, 57–59, 134

Hay, Eduardo, 130–131

Herzog, Jesus Silva, 94, 97–98, 100–101, 104, 107, 117

Hull, Cordell, 127–129, 131–132, 141

Icaza, Xavier, 114, 117–118

Illegal Cessation of Work, 106

Labor Unions, Beginnings of, 10, 61–63, 65–67
  Contract of 1936, 21, 73–78, 83
  C.R.O.M., 65–68
  C.T.M., 67–68, 70, 82 ,117
  "Exclusion Clause," 69, 79, 81
  "Grandmother Clause," 78, 109
  Management Clauses, 75–76, 79, 83, 101, 107, 111–112, 115
  Petroleum Workers' Union, 69, 73, 83, 86, 116

Mexican Bar Association, 120

Mexican Bonds, 15–16, 19, 30, 117, 125–126

Mexican Petroleum Company, 29–30, 39

Monroe Doctrine, 2, 11, 127, 141, 143

Morones, Luis, 65, 67

Morrow, Dwight, 18, 60

National Mixed Commission, 109

Obregón, Alvaro, 14–17, 54, 56, 72, 140

Oil Companies, Objections to Experts' Award, 101–102
Objections to Group Seven Award, 113, 119
Offers to Compromise, 83–86, 115
Profits, 47–48, 50, 78, 93, 97–99, 101, 107
Questionnaire to Union Experts, 104–105
Refusal of Cardenas' Terms of Payment, 134
Tribute to Bandits, 16, 45–46, 116
Oil Lands, Acquisition of, 29, 30, 35
Oil Sales to Totalitarian Nations, 136–137, 143
"Positive Acts," 56, 60
Protests by Dutch and British, 21, 125–126
Rebeldía, Definition and Distortion of, 119, 121
Robinson, A. A., 26–28
Silver, 4–5, 124, 133
Six-Year-Plan, 20, 67
Social Benefits, 38, 40–42, 48, 51, 74, 77, 86, 101, 104, 108–110
Decrease after Expropriation, 138

Socialists, 10, 62–63, 66
Spanish "Law of Reversion," 31–34
Subsoil Rights, 13, 18, 30–35, 51, 53
Supreme Court of Mexico, 21, 55, 82, 112–115, 117–119, 123
Labor Court, 114, 117
Labor Court "Draft of Decision," 118
Syndicalists, 10, 62–63, 65
Taxes, 16–17, 29, 45, 49, 51, 56, 60, 72, 120, 124, 133
Toledano, Vicente Lombardo, 20–21, 67–68, 79–80, 82, 93–94, 114, 116–117, 120
Trotsky, Leon, 19
U.S. Department of State, 2, 15, 17–18, 46, 53, 66, 81, 116, 127–128, 132–134
Notes to Mexico, 22, 127–129, 131–132
Wages, 21, 41, 45, 48, 51, 70, 73–75, 77–78, 85–86, 93, 97, 100–101, 107–108, 110, 111
Decrease after Expropriation, 138–139
Zapata, 10, 13

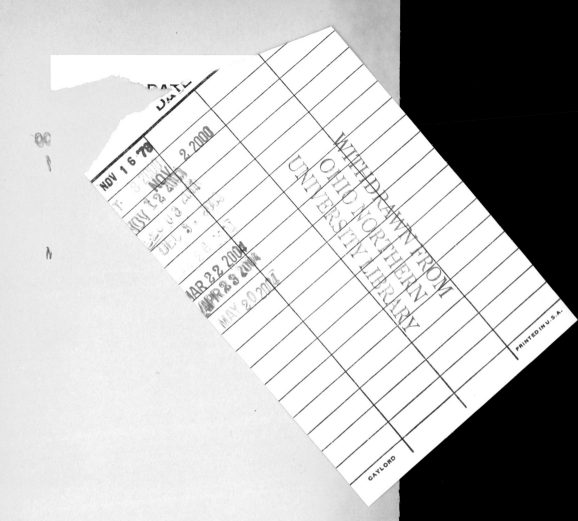